Called, Equipped & No Place to Go: Women Pastors and the Church

By

Randal Huber

Copyright © 2003 by Warner Press/Church of God Ministries, Inc
ISBN 1-59317-021-1

Unless otherwise noted, all scripture quotations are from the
New Revised Standard Version of the Bible, copyright 1989
by the Division of Christian Education of the
National Council of the Churches of Christ in the USA
and used by permission.

All Rights Reserved
Printed in the United States of America

Arthur Kelly, Publishing Coordinator and Editor

Cover and Layout by
Curtis D. Corzine and Virginia L. Wachenschwanz

WOMEN PASTORS:
A Biblical Perspective

Dedication

With deepest gratitude in my heart to the Lord Jesus Christ, I dedicate this project to the glory of God and to the two special women who have enriched my life beyond words. To my mother, Janice Elaine Huber, who went home to be with the Lord on March 29, 2001—I thank you for bringing me into this world, for nurturing me in the faith, and for fanning my ministerial calling into flame. To my faithful and supportive wife Susan—I thank you for standing by my side for over twenty-six years of marriage and for ministering by my side all of my adult life. This book and nearly every other accomplishment of my life would have been unattainable without your love and prayers.

Acknowledgements

This project would have been impossible without the faithful and insightful contributions of John Stanley, Susie Stanley, Beth Harness McCracken, Sharon Clark Pearson, and Juanita Leonard. I also deeply appreciate the consistent and heartfelt support of the Anderson University School of Theology faculty. I will be forever grateful for the spiritual, emotional, and financial support of Chapel Hill Church of God whom I have served as senior pastor for over twenty years. Special thanks are due to Peter Hobbs who created a database to aid me in my survey work. He labored sacrificially to help me gather data. Peter understands technology in ways that amaze me and his contribution is beyond estimation. I also want to thank my Chapel Hill Church of God local support team, Ted Decker, Kim Isaac, Mike LeMay, Jeannine Slaybaugh, and Harold Wantz for their encouragement and many helpful suggestions. Thanks are also due to William Burcher, Judy Cobb, and John Stanley who have met regularly with me as my professional development team. Mere words cannot express my gratitude for the invaluable help that all these persons have contributed to this project.

A Note to Readers

The persons who "write" to me at the beginning of each of chapter of this book are fictitious. They represent males and females of diverse ethnic and racial backgrounds. They represent both the educated and those who have no formal training. They come from different movements and denominations. Any resemblance to real persons is purely incidental and unintentional.

I have included discussion questions at the end of each chapter. You might want to personally consider them as you read. Feel free to use them for discussion in pulpit and search committees, college classrooms, Sunday school classes, and small groups.

CONTENTS

Open Hearts, Open Minds 7

Gifts not Gender 15

He Shall Rule Over You 23

A Men's Club 32

A Sexist Savior 40

Paul Says 50

I'm a Stay-at-Home Mom 66

A Woman Couldn't Do It 78

A Modern Feminist Thing 96

A Sin Against God 103

End Notes 114

Selected Bibliography 116

Appendix A: Questionnaire for Female Church of God Ministers 132

Appendix B: Overall Survey Response 135

General Index 136

Biographical Index 141

Scriptures Index 144

OPEN HEARTS, OPEN MINDS
A Personal Journey

Despite hours of prayer and seemingly endless meetings, the pastoral search committee was no closer to finding a new pastor than when they first began. Again and again, they reassured one another, "God has prepared just the right pastor for this congregation." The reality was that God did not seem to be leading them to call anyone. They were frustrated and discouraged. Pressure was intensifying as the congregation was treading water. Some persons were leaving and concerned members kept asking, "When are we going to have our new pastor?" Finally, one member of the committee raised an uncomfortable subject. He said, "We have dozens of ministerial resumes from women. Why haven't we seriously considered any of these? Could it be that God wants a woman to be our next pastor?"

Is it biblical for women to be pastors? Can women effectively lead the church? Some teach that women are permanently disqualified from church leadership. They believe God put men in charge and that women must be forever subordinate to them. I believe the Bible, rightly understood, allows all qualified persons to serve as leaders in the church. It is time for the church to fully recognize and utilize the gifts of called and equipped women.

You may already have a negative opinion about women in church leadership but are you willing to consider another perspective? Timothy P. Weber notes: "There are people on both sides of this question who will not change their minds no matter how cogent or persuasive the exegetical arguments because they personally have too much at stake in the outcome" (Mickelsen, 1986:282). Some denominations, such as the Southern Baptist Convention and the Roman Catholic Church prohibit women from serving at any levels of ministerial leadership. It takes courageous souls to buck those prevailing views.

I recognize that presenting a convincing case for women pastors is an uphill climb. Women pastors are not, and never have been, in the majority. Perhaps you were raised in a church that taught against women pastors. You trust those who taught you. You are confident they would not knowingly mislead you. Even if you were raised in a church that has historically affirmed the call of women pastors, you may not personally know even one woman pastor. If you know your Bible you can point to some Bible texts that seem to clearly suggest male headship. You can easily build a theology that keeps women subordinate to men. You can make a case from history. Males have predominantly led the Christian church for centuries. You may have ambiguity about women in authority. You may not feel comfortable with a female leader. Maybe you don't believe women should even work outside of the home. As you read with an open heart and an open mind, sometimes you may be shouting "Amen!" At other times you may squirm; "But that is not what I have been taught!" It takes courage to honestly examine your treasured beliefs.

We Discover the Truth in the Bible

I am a committed believer in the Bible. The Bible is inspired by God and is our infallible guide for faith and life (2 Tim 3:16, 2 Pet 1:20-21). We need to take the Bible very seriously. As you and I study the Bible we will be moving beyond a surface literal reading of it. There is a difference between being biblically literal and being biblically literate. C. S. Cowles suggests seven principles of biblical interpretation that will guide us in our study (1993:32–37).

First, "we must see what the text actually says" (1993:33). This sometimes requires that we look beyond the English translation to explore the original Greek and Hebrew. For example, when we consider Paul's mention of Phoebe in Romans 16 should the rendering of the Greek *diakonos* be *servant, minister,* or *deacon?* We are sometimes influenced by the words translators have selected when other words might better capture the meaning of the original text.

Second, "we must take careful note of the immediate context of a scriptural passage" (1993:33). For example, instructions about the role of women in 1 Timothy 2:11–12 must be understood within the cultural context of 1 Timothy. Elements of the second chapter, for example, deal with specific cultural issues such as how to live as subjects of a king, women's fashion, and childbirth. Every biblical passage is set within a context that affects how we should understand and apply it.

Third, "a particular passage must be evaluated in the larger context of all that a particular author has to say, as well as the intention and purpose of the Bible in its entirety" (1993:33). For example, difficult texts such as 1 Corinthians 14:33–36 and 1 Timothy 2:11–12 need to be understood in the light of Paul's other teachings and practices. Paul readily accepted the ministry of women and in Galatians 3:28 Paul proclaimed the equality of women.

Fourth, "we must distinguish between what is *descriptive* and what is *prescriptive* in the Bible" (1993:35). Many things are truthfully described in scripture that God does not necessarily prescribe as godly or appropriate practices. For example the Bible describes various rapes. That doesn't mean that God prescribes rape as a godly activity. The Bible describes how men would come to rule over women as a consequence of sin. That doesn't mean that God prescribes that men rule over women.

Fifth, "we need to recognize the difference between the *particular* and the *universal*, between what is historically conditioned and what is timeless truth" (1993:35). For example, most Christians today do not require women to wear veils when they pray or preach, but veils were expected in a first century Grecian city like Corinth.

Sixth, "we need to be fully aware of the historical, social, and cultural context that forms the background of a given scripture" (1993:36). Looking again at the veil issue, women wore veils to demonstrate that they were married. To discard the veil in the first century is somewhat analogous to modern women choosing to discard their wedding rings. Likewise, 1 Timothy was written to Timothy, the leader of the church at Ephesus. The Ephesian church wrestled with false teachers and emerging gnosticism.

Finally, seventh, "we must distinguish between God's original intentions for us and His accommodation to our fallen estate" (1993:36). For example, God prescribed monogamous marriage yet blessed several holy persons, such as Jacob and David, who practiced polygamy.

I am asking you to prayerfully study this book. Each person brings his or her background, experiences, and assumptions to interpreting the Bible.

Wesleyans have historically affirmed that we come to understand truth by interpreting scripture in the light of reason, tradition, and experience. Susie Stanley notes: "They are not equally important. The Bible is the primary source of theological authority, followed by experience. Tradition and reason have a place, but they play lesser roles compared to Scripture and experience" (2002:18). I am asking you to test the contents of this book against scripture, reason, tradition, and experience. Pray. Think.

My Journey through Change

Careful study has challenged me to change my beliefs. I grew up as an Episcopalian. From the time I was twelve years old, I experienced God's call to become an Episcopal priest. I loved the Episcopal Church. It was all I knew and the wonderful people of my local parish affirmed my call to ministry. In the 1960s the Episcopal Church had no female bishops or priests. It just didn't seem biblical or proper. Jesus was a man. The twelve apostles were men. When challenged about an all-male hierarchy, my male priests would point to selected verses in the Apostle Paul's letters. It was clear; God only called men into the priesthood. For centuries, only men led the Episcopal Church. As a lifetime Episcopalian, I was comfortable with an all-male hierarchy. It was all that I knew. In the 1960s, some forward thinking Episcopal Bible scholars and leaders were seriously examining the issue of ordaining women but this issue wasn't even a faint blip on my personal radarscope.[1]

In the mid 1970s God called me out of the Episcopal Church and into the Church of God (Anderson). It was a remarkable and moving experience for me. In the middle of singing a hymn at Trinity Anglican Church in Barrie, Ontario, God spoke to me. A voice deep in my soul said: "Randy, I don't want you here." I began to weep and asked, "But where Lord, where do you want me?" God answered, "Don't worry, I'm with you and I'll show you." By faith I left the church that had nurtured my faith for nineteen years. Within a couple of months God drew me into the Church of God. I poured over the Bible reevaluating my entire theology. It was a huge leap from a mainline liturgical church to the Church of God.

During this intensive rethinking of my faith I did not give much thought to women pastors. It didn't seem important. To put it bluntly, I am male and the issue of women in ministry had no relevance for me. Males have always been accepted as pastors and I did not know a single female that had claimed that God called her into ministry. That changed when I entered seminary at

Anderson University School of Theology. Every day in classes I came to know and appreciate highly gifted women who believed that God had called them into church leadership. Their gifts were obvious and who was I to argue against their personal experiences of God's call? Still I inwardly had to ask, "Is it biblical for women to be pastors and church leaders?" Over a period of three years in seminary I began to comprehend a persuasive biblical case for women pastors, but I had more pressing issues on my mind. I had to learn how to lead a church, how to preach biblical sermons, and how to conduct weddings and funerals. The issue of women in ministry was on a back burner as I closed my seminary days and gained experience in my first pastorate in London, Ontario.

In November of 1982 God called me to be pastor of Chapel Hill Church of God in York Springs, Pennsylvania. Chapel Hill is a rural congregation set in the heart of rolling hills and picturesque apple orchards. Women leaders laid the foundation of the church and have played a pivotal role throughout its history. In 1919 three women, Sisters Helpingstone, Smith and Wallace led revival services in the area. Two families accepted the truths of the Church of God and became the nucleus for a Bible study group that Sister Wallace led for one- and-a half years. In 1931 Chapel Hill Church of God located at its present location and built a small sanctuary. In 1936, the congregation sent their first missionary to Africa, a woman named Lima Lehmer.[2] Lima Lehmer's parents, Lyman and Mabel Lehmer attended Chapel Hill Church of God. Sister Flora Hinzman pastored the church from 1944–47. All through the years women served on the church council and were involved in leadership. Women formed the foundation of this wonderful congregation. All this changed abruptly around 1980. The church split. Many who left the congregation were those who understood the history and theology of the church. Many who remained came from evangelical and fundamentalist backgrounds. They believed, as I once believed, that the Bible forbids women to be pastors. They were unaware of the great role women played in founding the congregation. They were unaware that the Church of God has always ordained women pastors. They were unaware of any biblical case that endorsed women pastors. During a period of pastoral vacancy, the congregation changed the bylaws. The new bylaws forbade women to be pastors or elders in the congregation.

I arrived as pastor the same year those new bylaws went into effect. Encouraging women in ministry was not one of my high priorities. I was a green twenty-six year old pastor trying to help a congregation recover from a painful split. I said nothing about women in leadership until 1988 when we were evaluating our bylaws. The leadership at the time was not interested in opening ministry doors for women. At Chapel Hill we evaluate our bylaws every five years, so I approached the subject again in 1990 and 1995. In each case, I sensed resistance, backed away, and did not push. The male leaders were not ready to address women in ministry and I was not willing to risk too much on the issue. In 1995, we were considering calling an associate pastor. We had an outstanding resume from a woman. Some of our leaders did not feel comfortable calling a woman pastor and our bylaws forbade it anyway. I had the responsibility of phoning this woman and telling her that we were not considering her because of her sex. That was one of the most embarrassing phone calls of my life. I felt awful. I had come to appreciate a clear biblical case for women in ministry and yet I never adequately taught the congregation I served. I knew in my heart that it was not right. This godly, called, and equipped woman could not serve as an associate pastor in our church for one and only one reason. She was a woman. I apologized to her. She was gracious but even today I still feel ashamed. I knew the truth but did not act upon it. Around that same time, Doctors Susie and John Stanley made an appointment with me. They were concerned that I should take a stand on women in ministry. As I listened, I knew they were right. God was in it. The Bible affirmed what they were asking and the timing seemed right. I promised, "I will go to the wall on it." A short time later, I preached eleven sermons on Women of the Faith. I preached about creation and the fall, Miriam and Deborah, Anna and Phoebe. I explored Jesus' treatment of women and what Paul had to say.

The church showed great maturity. They had open hearts and minds. Shortly after the series, they changed our bylaws so that women could be pastors and elders. They warmly accepted a female summer intern. They have enjoyed different women speakers who have preached when I have been away. A woman in our congregation was recently ordained. We now have a female elder on our board who also serves as chairperson of our board of elders and chairperson of our congregation. Several of our growth group pastors are women. The church is also making room for women in other positions of leadership.

In the late 1990's Dr. John Stanley and I did some speaking around the country. We wrote a booklet called, *Reclaiming the Wesleyan/Holiness Heritage of Women Clergy.* The booklet contained eleven of my sermons, a seminar outline, and some helpful academic resources that John Stanley included. The Louisville Institute gave us a grant that enabled us to conduct seminars at the North American Convention of the Church of God in Anderson, Indiana; Point Loma Nazarene University, near San Diego; Eastern States Ministers Retreat in Pennsylvania; Warner Pacific College in Portland, Oregon; the Christian Holiness Partnership in Virginia Beach, Virginia; and finally the Wesleyan Theological Society and Mid-America Bible College, both in Oklahoma City, Oklahoma.

John and I repeatedly discovered that male pastors and key decision leaders are not inclined to attend meetings that have to do with women. Other subjects seem more pressing and relevant. I understand. I used to feel the same way. This book is my earnest effort to reach beyond a small group of interested women to address the wider church. It is part of my Doctoral Studies Program at Anderson University School of Theology. I am writing specifically for the Church of God but I pray that the message will reach far and wide. This issue crosses racial and ethnic lines. It crosses denominational and national boundaries. It is a biblical issue. I hope for a wide reading by women and men of all ethnic communities and from many denominations and nationalities, by pastors, district, state and national administrators, by educators, pulpit and pastoral search committees. I pray that God's people in the pews will use this book and study their Bibles with open hearts and open minds.

Discussion Questions for
A Personal Journey

1. Why is it difficult for persons to keep open hearts and open minds when discussing treasured opinions?

2. What factors in your experience have most affected your view of women pastors and leaders in the church?

3. Wesleyans sometimes speak of the "quadrilateral" of scripture, reason, tradition, and experience. Is it possible to interpret the Bible without being influenced by reason, tradition, and experience? Why or why not?

4. Why are the seven biblical interpretation principles put forth by C. S. Cowles essential to a proper understanding of the Bible?

5. What role does the Holy Spirit play in interpreting the Bible?

6. The author suggests that male pastors and decision-making leaders did not place priority on attending the seminars that he and Dr. John Stanley conducted throughout the United States. Why do you think women were more inclined than men to attend these "Reclaiming the Wesleyan/Holiness Heritage of Women Clergy" seminars?

7. Why is it essential that pulpit committees and decision-makers approach their Bibles with open hearts and open minds?

GIFTS NOT GENDER

Chapter 1

Brother Huber:
As you know, I have been part of the church all of my life. I'm faithful. I love the church. I believe the Bible and I love God. It's in my blood. My grandfather was a preacher and evangelist. My father has served as a church trustee for over forty years. He helped to build our church camp. I have served as a deacon, a trustee, an usher, and a Sunday school teacher. I do not say these things to brag. I just want you to know that I am a committed disciple of Jesus Christ, and I have a serious problem with what I heard you saying about women pastors.

I believe you are working against God in trying to make a case for women pastors. It's not that I believe women are stupid. Some of them are smarter than I am. It's not that God doesn't love women. God loves women as much as he loves men. Gender roles are the issue. It doesn't require a rocket scientist to recognize that men and women are different. God intended those differences. Men are physically stronger. Women are more easily deceived. God uses women one way and men another. God intends men to lead and women to follow. God gives different spiritual gifts to men and women. My wife is a wonderful caregiver. She visits the shut-ins in our church. My grandmother has given her life to our women's mission society. My sister is an artist in the kitchen. You have never tasted better gravy! My pastor is a powerful man with a commanding presence. He is *anointed with a spirit of prophecy. He speaks with authority. People naturally follow this great man of God. God does not gift women to preach or to lead men as my pastor leads.*

A woman may be highly capable but leadership in the church is for men alone. One time our family was traveling on vacation. We visited a church. The church seemed friendly enough but when we found out they had a woman leading worship, I made sure our family got out fast. We quickly drove to a more biblical congregation. Preaching also is for men alone. One time I was listening to a Christian radio station. They had a woman teaching the Bible. I shut that station off and sent a letter to the station management. God gives spiritual gifts according to sex. For men to listen to women preachers or teachers, or to submit to female authority in the church, is to go against God. Only men have the proper spiritual gifts. I pray that you will see the light.

May God bless you.

Deacon Charles

Dear Deacon Charles:

I applaud your faithfulness to God and the church. You have been blessed with a wonderful spiritual heritage. You and your family have made significant contributions to God's kingdom. I want to thank you for taking the time to share your thoughts with me.

You have raised some important questions. I will do my best to respond. I want to begin by defining some terms. Your view is what I call gender-based leadership. I call my view gifts-based leadership. I'm not implying that you don't believe in spiritual gifts. Those who take a gender-based view of leadership also believe in spiritual gifts. You certainly would agree no pastor should lead a church without godly character and the appropriate gifts. You would add that godly character and spiritual gifts are not enough. A person may be loaded with spiritual gifts, have godly character, excellent education and talent, but if she is a woman she cannot pastor. She cannot be an elder. She cannot teach men or exercise any form of authority over them. In your letter you added that you do not believe that God even gives the appropriate spiritual gifts to women. You believe leadership is gender-based.

I argue for gifts-based leadership. Godly called and gifted men and women are qualified for leadership. Godly character and spiritual gifts, not one's sex, are the factors that qualify a person for leadership. That is the crux of our disagreement. Leadership is based upon gifts, not sex. Joseph Allison notes that in the October 14, 1920 issue of *The Gospel Trumpet,* Church of God leader F. G. Smith wrote: "God's government is based upon divine gifts hence the only way to prove that a woman cannot hold a particular position is not by citing the mere fact that she is a woman, but you must prove that God does not give such gifts to women. If you can prove that, the subject is settled. But where will you go to prove it?" (1978:27). The Bible is the ultimate authority on all such matters. Is my position biblical?

Women Were Present as the Church Prayed and Conducted its Earliest Business

The Book of Acts tells the exciting account of the birth and growth of the early church. Following Jesus' ascension into heaven, Jesus' disciples gathered in an upper room. They waited in eager anticipation for Jesus' promised gift of the Holy Spirit. They were following Jesus' instructions. "While staying with them, he ordered them not to leave Jerusalem, but to wait there for the promise of the Father. 'This,' he said, 'is what you have heard from me; for John baptized with water, but you will be baptized with the Holy Spirit not many days from now'" (Acts 1:4–5). It wasn't just the twelve waiting in that upper room. Acts 1:15 tells us there were about one hundred twenty persons in those gatherings. Nor were all the persons men. "All these were constantly devoting themselves to prayer, together with certain women, including Mary, the mother of Jesus, as well as his brothers" (Acts 1:14). Women were present in the upper room as the church prayed and conducted its earliest business. Women were present as the church decided to replace Judas, the Lord's betrayer, with Matthias. Women were also present when God poured out the gift of the Holy Spirit upon the church. Acts 2 records, "When the day of Pentecost had come, they were all together in one place. And suddenly from heaven there came a sound like the rush of a violent wind, and it filled the entire house where they were sitting" (Acts 2:1–2).

Both Men and Women Received the Holy Spirit and Were Gifted to Prophesy

The biblical texts make it clear there were women present at the first outpouring of the Holy Spirit upon the church. The Acts 2 experience of receiving the Holy Spirit directly follows the notation that women were present in

Acts 1:14. Acts 2:1 says they were "all together in one place." *All* means *all*. About one hundred and twenty women and men received the Holy Spirit. Not only did they receive the Holy Spirit but they all received the gift of speaking in foreign languages. Again note the word *all*. "All of them were filled with the Holy Spirit and began to speak in other languages, as the Spirit gave them ability" (Acts 2:4). God poured out the Holy Spirit on men and women. There was no distinction on the basis of sex. If there is any doubt that women also received the gift of the Holy Spirit, consider the passage from Joel that Peter quoted to explain the incredible phenomena of persons hearing men and women praising God in their own languages.

Now this is what was spoken through the prophet Joel: "In the last days it will be, God declares, that I will pour out my Spirit upon all flesh, and your sons and your daughters shall prophesy, and your young men shall dream dreams. Even upon my slaves, both men and women, in those days I will pour out my Spirit; and they shall prophesy" (Acts 2:16–18).

God poured out the gift of the Holy Spirit upon *all flesh.* Both men and women were gifted to prophesy. In fact, when Peter quotes Joel he adds the word *prophesy* a second time, emphasizing the task the Holy Spirit enabled.

One could scarcely overestimate the impact of this text. To prophesy is to speak the word of God. The most common expression of prophecy today is inspired and anointed preaching. The Apostle Paul proclaims prophecy as one of the greatest gifts.

> Pursue love and strive for spiritual gifts, and especially that you may prophesy. For those who speak in a tongue do not speak to other people but to God; for nobody understands them, since they are speaking mysteries in the Spirit. On the other hand, those who prophesy speak to other people for their up building and encouragement and consolation. Those who speak in a tongue build up themselves, but those who prophesy build up the church. Now I would like all of you to speak in tongues, but even more to prophesy. One who prophesies is greater than one who speaks in tongues, unless someone interprets, so that the church may be built up (1 Cor 14:1–5).

Note the incredible impact of this text upon women as preachers in the church. We already know from the Acts 2:16–18 text that in these last days God empowers women and men to prophesy. Paul's instruction in this text is that all should seek to prophesy. Speaking God's word to the church, edifies, encourages, and consoles. This lofty and important gift of speaking God's word to the church is a gift for "all," for men and for women. Women and men have the awesome responsibility of speaking God's word so that "the church may be built up." Whether spoken by a woman or a man, the Word of God itself has authority upon its hearers.

The testimony of Acts 1—2 is that God poured out the Holy Spirit upon women as well as men. All spoke in foreign languages. People gathered in Jerusalem from all over the Middle East heard these women and men proclaiming the "mighty deeds of God" (Acts 2:5–11). Peter's response to the skeptics, quoting the prophet Joel, was that women and men would receive the Holy Spirit and prophesy. To prophesy is to speak forth the word of God. To prophesy is to preach. These prophets would "build up" the church by speaking the prophetic word of God. I have searched the New Testament for any indication that God gives different gifts to men and women and concur with Marianne Meye Thompson's conclusion, "Nowhere does the New Testament say that God gives gifts on the basis of gender" (Mickelsen, 1986:93).

Both Men and Women are a New Creation and Entrusted as Ambassadors

Clearly, men and women are equally gifted by God and given responsibility in the church and for the world. Consider 2 Corinthians 5:16–20.

> From now on, therefore, we regard no one from a human point of view, Even though we once knew Christ from a human point of view, we know him no longer in that way. So if anyone is in Christ, there is a new creation: everything old has passed away; see everything has become new! All this is from God, who reconciled us to himself through Christ, and has given us the ministry of reconciliation; that is in Christ God was reconciling the world to himself, not counting their trespasses against them, and entrusting the message of reconciliation to us. So we are ambassadors for Christ, since God is making his appeal through us; we entreat you on behalf of Christ, be reconciled to God (2 Cor 5:16–20).

Are only men a new creation? Are only men Christ's ambassadors? Are only men entrusted with the message of reconciliation? "We regard no one from a human point of view." All members of the church, women and men, are Christ's ambassadors. Sex does not disqualify women from being ambassadors for Christ. We all make the appeal to "be reconciled to God." To be an ambassador is to bear the high privilege of speaking on behalf of the one who sent you. Women and men are ambassadors of the Lord Jesus Christ. Gretchen Gaebelin Hull, who makes a strong case for women in ministry, writes:

> This word ambassador is a strong word in the original New Testament Greek, just as it is in English. It means the highest official envoy, someone accredited to go to a foreign government as representative of his or her own government. In Greek, it comes from the same family of words as the word elder or overseer. Ambassador denotes an important, authoritative role, and it is a role all believers are called to fill (1995:4).

Women and men both have important functions in the church's life and ministry.

The Church is a Body That Needs the Gifts of Both Men and Women

The Apostle Paul compares the church to a body. Three key texts refer to the use of spiritual gifts in the body of Christ. Those texts are Romans 12:4–8, 1 Corinthians 12:4–26, and Ephesians 4:11–12. Grace Ying May and Hyunhye Pkrifka Joe write:

> To restrict women's gifts is to disobey God. The New Testament teaching about gifts always occurs in the context of a discussion of the interdependence of Christ's body. The Spirit assigns gifts to women and men for the explicit purpose of enriching their common life. It is our gifts, not our sex that determines our function in the body (1997:9).

Every member of the body, whether male or female, has a God-given role in the church. God wants his body to be an authentic community of men and women, young and old, people from all nations, races and social classes. Each one is to exercise his or her spiritual gifts for the common good. In an interview with Lauren Winner, Gilbert Bilezikian, states, "And authentic community necessarily implies full participation of women and men on the basis of spiritual gifts, not on the basis of sex" (2000:58).

Leadership in the church is based upon spiritual gifts, not upon sex. Richard Goode wrote, "Obedience, not gender is the standard. If the Holy Spirit has called and equipped a woman for pastoral ministry, we dare not stand in her way. If we do, we are blocking the very work of God" (1989:19). Those who are gifted to preach should preach. Those who are gifted to teach should teach. Those who are gifted to lead should lead. I have been richly blessed as men and women have used their spiritual gifts in the church. Churches prosper as God's people are released to minister. The body of Christ is both male and female. God gives the gifts of the Spirit without distinction to males and females.

Deacon Charles, I used to believe some of the same things that you believe. Studying God's Word prompted me to change. I know that you love God and that you are committed to scripture. I believe the texts that I have shared with you show that God does gift women to preach. If you still have questions or concerns please feel free to write back to me. We can continue our discussion and consider some other biblical texts. As we share, I'm sure that we can learn from one another. I wish you God's blessing.

In Christian Love,

Brother Huber

Discussion Questions for Chapter 1

1. Why is it significant that both women and men were present when the early church was making its earliest decisions?

2. Why is it significant that God poured out the Holy Spirit upon both women and men?

3. Since God has empowered women to prophesy, that is, to speak the word of God, how does preventing women from exercising their spiritual gifts as pastors and preachers affect God's anointing and blessing upon the church?

4. Hull said, "Ambassador denotes an important, authoritative role, and it is a role all believers are called to fill." How does the fact that both women and men are Christ's ambassadors address the argument that women should not have authority?

5. In what ways are those who teach gender-based leadership hindering the body of Christ from experiencing the benefits of all the gifts in the body?

6. What do you think of the Grace Ying May and Hyunhye Pkrifka Joe quote: "To restrict women's gifts is to disobey God"?

HE SHALL RULE OVER YOU

Chapter 2

Dear Randy:

   I pray that God is prospering your ministry. I value the friendship that we have enjoyed so many years. We agree on most things and we have much in common. We both have attended college and seminary. We both pastor a good church. We both have pastored outside of the United States, you in Canada and me in Mexico. We both love the Lord. I know that your heart is right but I am concerned about the stand you are taking on women in ministry. It seems to me that you are disregarding important biblical texts. This women in ministry issue means a great deal to you and I don't want to hurt you but in the interest of truth I feel compelled to share my views.

   I want to focus on the book of Genesis. The book of Genesis clearly shows that God created men to rule over women. Note that God created Adam first. By being first, Adam is clearly preeminent. Later God created Eve as a helper. "Then the LORD God said, 'It is not good that the man should be alone; I will make him a helper as his partner'" (Gen 2:18). Adam is in charge. Eve is the helper. To show her intrinsic subordinate role look at Genesis 2:21–22. "So the LORD God caused a deep sleep to fall upon the man, and he slept; then he took one of his ribs and closed up its place with flesh. And the rib that the LORD God had taken from the man he made into a woman and brought her to the man." The woman was taken from the man. She is derived from him and thus draws her identity *and worth from him. If there is any doubt that God intended for the man to be in charge look at Genesis 3. As you know, this is God's curse on the woman after the fall. "To the woman he said, 'I will greatly increase your pangs in childbearing; in pain you shall bring forth children, yet your desire shall be for your husband, and he shall rule over you'" (Gen 3:16).*

Furthermore, the Genesis account makes it clear that women are more prone to be deceived than men are and are thus less fit to lead.

Randy, when you teach that women can preach or pastor you are ignoring what God established in creation. At creation, God intended men to be in charge. I hope that you will consider these texts. As always, I value your friendship.

In His Name,

Carlos

Dear Carlos,

It was great to hear from you. I also value our friendship. Thank you for taking the time to share your views with me. I have spoken with others who believe as you do. As you may remember, I used to believe that way too. Carlos, I know your heart. I also appreciate your many years of study and education but I believe that you need to explore this matter more deeply. Your viewpoint appears unassailable but these issues require more serious examination of the texts. I believe you are making some faulty assumptions and inferences. You are also missing the awesome impact of Genesis 1.

No Hierarchy between Men and Women at Creation

As I respond, I will demonstrate that there is no hierarchy whatsoever between men and women at creation. The many problems occur after the fall. Look carefully at Genesis 1:26–28.

> Then God said, "Let us make humankind in our image, according to our likeness; and let them have dominion over the fish of the sea, and over the birds of the air, and over the cattle, and over all the wild animals of the earth, and over every creeping thing that creeps upon the earth." So God created humankind in his image, in the image of God he created them; male and female he created them. God blessed them,

and God said to them, "Be fruitful and multiply, and fill the earth and subdue it; and have dominion over the fish of the sea and over the birds of the air and over every living thing that moves upon the earth."

Note first of all that both the man and the woman are created in God's likeness. This is repeated in Genesis 5:1–2. Both are created in the image of God. The woman is not the man's appendage finding her identity in the man. She is also created in the likeness of God. The commands to be fruitful, to subdue the earth, and to have dominion are given to "them." God creates both the male and the female in the divine image and gives both the male and the female dominion. There is no hierarchy. There is no distinction whatever. The man is not put in charge. The male and the female are equal before God. Gilbert Bilezikian makes a strong case affirming the equality of women and men at creation. I heartily concur with him as he writes:

> In the Genesis 1 account of God's creation design, neither maleness or femaleness connotes a disparity in rank or function. Both man and woman bear the image of God, so their sexuality is the reflection of different aspects of the Creator's personality as a result, they both share equally the God assigned task of creation rulership without any intimation of role distinctions (1985:26).

Carlos, in your letter you indicated that because the man was created first in the Genesis 2 account, he clearly has supremacy over the woman. There is a serious flaw in this reasoning. "Temporal primacy of itself does not confer superior rank" (Bilezikian, 1985:30). Think for a moment. If being created first, confers rank, then Adam is inferior to all of the plants and animals that preceded him. The point is not who came first. The point is both man and woman are created in God's likeness and God gave both equal dominion over the earth.

You next misunderstand the meaning of the word *helper* in Genesis 2:18. The English word *helper* does not convey the rich meaning of the Hebrew. "Then the LORD God said, 'It is not good that the man should be alone; I will make him a helper as his partner" (Gen 2:18). You see a "helper" as an inferior. The original Hebrew does not support that view. Thompson notes the Hebrew *ezer kenegdo* means "a helper of his like" (Mickelsen, 1986:96). The idea is a counterpart to oneself. "The Hebrew language has four other words for 'helper' that denote subordination. None of those words is used in reference to women in Genesis 2" (Bilezikian, 1985:217). There is no hierarchy or subordination implied in the word *ezer kenegdo*. *Ezer kenegdo* is used nineteen times in the Old Testament. Fifteen times it is used of God who brings comfort to suffering people (Evans, 1983:16). One reference is Psalm 146:5. "Happy are those whose help is the God of Jacob, whose hope is in the LORD their God." Do we want to imply that God our "helper" is inferior or subordinate to the people God has made? It makes no sense to imply that the word *helper* implies the woman is inferior to the man. If the man needed a helper in this sense, it is the man who is inadequate. I don't argue for the inferiority or superiority of the man or the woman. In reality, both male and female need one another. At creation, God intended men and women to be equal partners. They complement and complete one another.

Carlos, you next suggest that Eve is somehow inferior to Adam because God created her from Adam's rib. You are missing the point of the narrative. The point is that out of all of the animals not one was "one like" Adam. Not one was a suitable *ezer kenegdo* who could complement and complete him. The fact that God created Eve from Adam's rib demonstrates that Adam and Eve come from the same flesh. They are made of the same substance. They are identical in nature. Together they are one flesh created in the image of God. Thompson writes:

> What is her derived creation intended to imply? First, it shows that she alone of all God's created subjects is a fit companion for man; thus it comes after God has brought all the animals to Adam and none is "fit" or "appropriate for him." Second, woman's derived creation explains the bonds of marriage; woman was created from man; from one come two. In marriage they are united once more into one flesh; two become one (Mickelsen, 1986:95–96).

There is no hierarchy in God's plan for men and women. "There is no justification for the derivation of Eve from the body of Adam to be viewed as a sign of subordination to him." Being made from one body "… demonstrates the essential identity between woman and man" (Bilezikian, 1985:29). God's original intent for men and women in marriage is a complimentary partnership. God wills for the two to become one flesh as they came from one flesh.

Marriage is not an unequal partnership. There is no difference of rank or nature between man and woman in Genesis chapters one and two. Our creator created males and females in the divine image and gave them dominion over the earth. Man and woman are of one flesh and nature. They complement and complete one another. They were placed in the garden and lived in complementary harmony, naked and unashamed.

Both Men and Women are Capable of Being Deceived and Being Rebellious

Temptation brought complications to paradise. The tempter deceived Eve and she ate the forbidden fruit. Eve offered the fruit to Adam and he deliberately rebelled against God. For centuries, some commentators have inferred from the fall that women are intrinsically more easily deceived than men. For this reason they are not fit to lead. You expressed this belief in your letter to me. It is true that the serpent deceived Eve but it is a major stretch to infer from that one deception that women are inherently more easily deceived than men. The text makes it clear that God directly informed Adam not to eat the forbidden fruit. "And the Lord God commanded the man, 'You may freely eat of every tree of the garden; but of the tree of the knowledge of good and evil you shall not eat, for in the day that you eat of it you shall die'" (Gen 2:16–17). With this knowledge clear in his mind, Adam willfully disobeyed God. Should we infer from that one rebellion that men are inherently more rebellious and inclined to sin than women are? Should we conclude since men are intrinsically more rebellious they are unfit to lead? Such inferences are equally unwarranted.

Carlos, you know the danger of over generalization. The truth is both men and women are capable of being deceived and both men and women are capable of rebelling against God. Personal experience and human history bear this out. The Apostle Paul, a male, describes himself as being deceived by sin (Rom 7:11). Likewise there is no shortage of women who have willfully disobeyed God. Jezebel, for example, set out to murder the godly prophet, Elijah (1 Kings 19:1–2). Satan is capable of deceiving and tempting both men and women.

While I am addressing the issue of Satan's temptations consider another thought. If there was a hierarchy in Adam and Eve's relationship before the fall, why did Satan even bother with Eve? If the man was in charge and the woman was merely a submissive "helper," then when Satan approached Eve he clearly addressed the wrong party. Adam would have been the one who needed to sin in order for the race to fall. Eve would have been superfluous. If Adam were in charge and Eve were subordinate, why would Satan first tempt the subordinate person? Concurring with this line of reasoning, Bilezikian adds: "Adam's willingness to follow Eve's example and to take the fruit she gave him confirms the absence of predetermined roles in the garden" (1985:42). Either party could have eaten the fruit first. The reality in the fall is that Adam followed Eve's leadership. It could have gone either way because there was no hierarchy, up to that point in that first relationship.

The Fall Seriously Undermined God's Intentions for Women and Men

Look at God's proclamation in Genesis 3.

> To the woman he said, "I will greatly increase your pangs in childbearing; in pain you shall bring forth children, yet your desire shall be for your husband, and he shall rule over you." And to the man he said, "Because you have listened to the voice of your wife, and have eaten of the tree about which I commanded you, 'You shall not eat of it,' cursed is the ground because of you; in toil you shall eat of it all the days of your life; thorns and thistles it shall bring forth for you; and you shall eat the plants of the field. By the sweat of your face you shall eat bread until you return to the ground, for out of it you were taken; you are dust, and to dust you shall return" (Gen 3:16–19).

In this pronouncement God announced the consequences of sin. Adam's and Eve's sin. Sin brought many horrors into our world. It brought blame. Adam blamed Eve for his sins. Eve blamed the serpent. It brought shame. Adam and Eve hid from God and felt a need to cover themselves. Sin brought relational separation. It marked the end of paradise in the garden. Following the *fall* came disease, death, murder, drought, famine, war, racism, slavery, greed—and the subjugation of women. Within six generations to Lamech there was polygamy.

Carlos, you noted the curse upon the woman. In addition to increased pain in child bearing "… your desire shall be for your husband, and he shall rule over you." This curse is not God's creation intention for men and women. It is the horrible consequence of sin. Evans calls this proclamation a "predictive" statement (1983:20). It predicts what would happen as the result of sin. Men would labor by the sweat of their brows and would rule women. Sadly, many Jews and Christians have preached and taught the tragic consequence of sin as though it were the creation plan of God. They have confused descriptive and prescriptive truth.

The Bible describes many events and conditions that God does not prescribe. The Bible describes polygamy, slavery, adultery, murder, war, greed, and the subjugation of women. None of these horrors is God's intention for the human race. They are the consequences of sin.

> The fall brought great pain and misery into the world. The fall had spawned the twin evils of woman's suffering in labor and of man's laboring in suffering. As a result of Satan's work, man was now master over woman, just as the mother-ground was now master over man. For these reasons it is proper to regard both male domination and death as being antithetical to God's original intent in creation. The 'he shall rule over you' should not be viewed as prescribing God's will any more than death may be regarded as God's will for humans (Bilezikian, 1985:56).

The subjugation of women is an unfortunate consequence of sin. Many abuses have come with the subjugation of women. Women have been beaten, dominated, and used as sexual objects. They have been denied property rights and basic human rights. They have been treated as property. Today, they are still paid less than men for the same work. They have been denied the opportunity to vote and to exercise their spiritual gifts in the church. They have suffered the abuse of patriarchy and male domination. Not one hint of male dominance is evident at creation. All of these abuses appear as a consequence of sin. The Bible *describes* these consequences but it does not *prescribe* them. God has higher plans for men and women. Those plans were clear in paradise. To preach the consequences of sin as though they are the plan of God is to perpetuate a great evil upon the human race and especially upon women.

Patriarchy and the subjugation of women are deeply ingrained in human society and in the church but they are not God's plan. They grieve God just as adultery, slavery, and murder grieve God. It is difficult for modern persons to grasp how deeply patriarchy has affected women throughout history. Ancient genealogies followed the male line. Men had to have sons because only sons could carry on the family name (Deut 25:5–10). Sons received the inheritance. Women were purchased and owned as the possessions of their husbands. Only males were true Israelites and bore the covenantal marks of circumcision. Women were second-class persons in ancient times and in many respects still are. This is a grievous fall from God's intention for creation as demonstrated in the garden.

Carlos, I know that you do not condone all of the cruelties and indignities that have been perpetrated against women, but making women permanently subordinate to men is less than God's intent for creation. God created both men and women in the divine likeness. God gave them equal dominion over the earth. They were made like one another to complement and help one another. God intended that men and women should love one another intimately. There is no prescription for male dominance at creation. The "He shall rule over you" curse refers to the terrible consequence of sin and the fall. It is not the plan of God but, like death and suffering, it is the curse of sin.

Carlos, I really appreciate you caring enough about me to express your views. I hope that what I have written will prompt more discussion. It would be great if we can get an opportunity to talk soon. We have enjoyed some great talks over the years. You're special to me! God's blessings.

In Christian love, I am your friend and brother,

Randy

Discussion Questions for Chapter 2

1. When considering whether God allows women to be pastors, why is it significant that God created both women and men in the divine image and gave both dominion over the earth?

2. In what ways does the English word "helper" fail to describe the woman's actual roles?

3. Do you agree with the author that it is an "over generalization" to declare upon the basis of one event that women are intrinsically more easily deceived than men? Why or why not?

4. Do you agree with the author that a parallel inference that men are intrinsically more inclined to rebel against God is equally a faulty inference? Why or why not?

5. What is the difference between descriptive and prescriptive truth?

6. Why is it important that the subjugation of women, like polygamy, slavery, and death is a descriptive truth?

7. Patriarchy is deeply imbedded in human society. In what ways does patriarchy harm women?

A Men's Club

Chapter 3

Dear Reverend Huber:

My pastor, David Watts asked me to talk with you. For several months our congregation has been considering calling an associate pastor. That's good. We really need a good man, but now the search committee is considering a woman! Pastor Watts and I have been debating whether women can be spiritual leaders. I admit that in the New Testament, Priscilla might have been a leader but I have been arguing that in the Old Testament all of the leaders are men. When I think of the Old Testament, I think of Abraham, Isaac, Jacob, Joseph, Moses, Joshua, Samson, David, Isaiah, Jeremiah, and Ezekiel. You know. They're all men. God clearly intended for men to be in charge. It's just in the nature of things. Pastor Watts said you have been studying this question and so he asked me to write you. I'm saying that leadership in the Old Testament is a men's club. What do you say?

Sincerely,

Jamal Smithson

Dear Jamal,

You and your pastor have been having an important conversation. This may surprise you, but I agree that in many ways Old Testament leadership was a men's club. The same thing is true in the New Testament. In fact, when you look globally at cultures over all periods of history, men have dominated the leadership positions. In rare instances we read of matriarchal societies but male dominance is firmly entrenched all over the world. This male dominance is the unfortunate result of institutionalized patriarchy. It goes back to the consequences of sin in the story of the Fall in Genesis 3.

Women Have Been Oppressed For Centuries

No thinking person can deny that women have been oppressed for centuries. C. S. Cowles notes an example in Africa. "When missionaries, as recently as the turn of the twentieth century, suggested that farmers could increase their yield of their fields by utilizing oxen to pull their plows, the tribesman protested that the cattle should not be used to do women's work" (1993:42).

Rosalind Miles notes that, "As late as 1921, the British Government Official Census of India recorded that 3,200,000 child-brides had died during the previous twelve months" (2001:112). Many of these ravaged girls were as young as eight years old. These girls lived and died having been given the sole purpose of satisfying the men in their lives.

Cowles quotes sixth century Greek philosopher Pythagoras: "There is a good principle which created order, light and man, and an evil principle which created chaos, darkness and woman" (1993:43). In the Old Testament, "A Jewish woman had the legal status of a slave and was regarded as a possession of her father and then of her husband. She had no legal rights of her own" (Cowles, 1993:46). Evans notes: "In the Old Testament as a whole, woman after the Fall, is seen as secondary" (1983:32). Leonard Swidler elaborates:

> … that the status of women in Rabbinic Judaism is predominantly negative.
>
> … In the daily prayers prescribed for Jewish males there is a threefold thanksgiving which graphically illustrated where women stood in Rabbinic Judaism: "Praised be God that he has not made me a gentile; Praised be God that he has not created me a woman; praised be God that he has not created me an ignorant man" (*Tosephta Berakhoth* 7, 8).

... Who speaks much with a woman draws down misfortune on himself, neglects the words of the law, and finally earns hell (*Mishnah Aboth* 1, 5).

... It is well for those whose children are male, but ill for those whose children are female (*Talmud bKiddushin*).

... Even the most virtuous of women is a witch (*Mishnah Terum 15*) (1979:154–157).

Women have been used, despised, raped, murdered, ritually mutilated, and kept in subjugation to males all through history. In this oppressive patriarchal context, we would not expect a preponderance or even an equal number of women in leadership positions. Since the fall, leadership has been predominantly a men's club.

Patriarchy is Not God's Plan. Leadership Should Not Be Gender-Based.

When considering Old Testament evidence regarding leadership, here are the issues, as I understand them. Patriarchy is not God's plan for the human race and God does not intend that leadership should be gender-based.

Jamal, I firmly maintain that patriarchy is not God's design for the human race. When God created men and women he created them without a hierarchy. They both were created in the divine image and both were given dominion over the earth. They were created to complement and complete one another. There is no hint of patriarchy at creation. Male dominance and female subjugation are the result of sin. The Lord described sin's curse in Genesis 3:16. "To the woman he said, 'I will greatly increase your pangs in childbearing; in pain you shall bring forth children, yet your desire shall be for your husband, and *he shall rule over you*'" (emphasis added). Male domination and patriarchy are the unfortunate result of the fall. Regrettably, most cultures in all of history have taught male domination as God's creation design. They have confused the Bible's *description* of patriarchy as God's *prescription* for patriarchy. In reality male domination is the tragic result of human sin.

Gender-based leadership clearly cannot be God's intent in the Old Testament. First, there is no evidence of gender-based leadership at creation. Second, if gender-based leadership were God's intent, why did God call and equip women to be spiritual leaders in Israel? Let's quickly examine four examples: Miriam, Deborah, Huldah, and Anna.

Miriam—Prophet and Leader of God's People

You remember that Miriam was Moses' and Aaron's sister. The Israelites were overwhelmed with praise when God conquered their enemies and led them safely through the sea. Exodus 15:20–21 records: "Then the prophet Miriam, Aaron's sister, took a tambourine in her hand; and all the women went out after her with tambourines and with dancing. And Miriam sang to them: "Sing to the LORD, for he has triumphed gloriously; horse and rider he has thrown into the sea." Here Miriam is called a prophet. A prophet is a person who speaks God's word. The most common expression of prophecy is inspired preaching. Miriam also led the women in worship. Miriam was clearly one of the spiritual leaders of the people. Looking back upon the Exodus events, Micah 6:4 says, "For I brought you up from the land of Egypt, and redeemed you from the house of slavery; and I sent before you Moses, Aaron, and Miriam." Catherine Booth, co-founder of the Salvation Army, notes, "God here classes Miriam with Moses and Aaron, and declares that He sent her before His people" (1859:15). Moses was a leader. Aaron was a leader. Miriam was a leader. God sent them all forth as leaders. If God disqualifies women from spiritual leadership on the basis of gender, why did God call, equip, and use Miriam as a prophet and leader?

Deborah—God's Choice to Lead the Nation

Let's consider Deborah. We find Deborah's story in Judges 4 and 5. Judges 4:1–5 records:

> The Israelites again did what was evil in the sight of the LORD, after Ehud died. So the LORD sold them into the hand of King Jabin of Canaan, who reigned in Hazor; the commander of his army was Sisera, who lived in Harosheth-ha-goiim. Then the Israelites cried out to the LORD for help; for he had nine hundred chariots of iron, and had oppressed the Israelites cruelly twenty years. At that time Deborah, a prophetess, wife of Lappidoth, was judging Israel. She used to sit under the palm of Deborah between Ramah and Bethel in the hill country of Ephraim; and the Israelites came up to her for judgment.

Catherine Booth notices two things about this text. "First, the authority of Deborah as a prophetess, or revealer of God's will to Israel, was acknowledged and submitted to as implicitly as in the cases of the male judges who succeeded her. Secondly, she is made the military head of ten thousand men, Barak refusing to go to battle without her" (1859:14). This is a strong text for gifts-based leadership. The Israelites were suffering cruel oppression at the hands of the Canaanites. The people needed a leader. How did Deborah get her job? She wasn't elected by popular vote. Israel was no democracy. She wasn't a princess who inherited power from a deceased father. Israel was not yet a monarchy. God called and equipped Deborah. The Lord chose her as a prophet and leader. She judged the people. She led the military. God chose Deborah to be the judicial, spiritual, and military leader of Israel. Even in a world twisted and marred by sin and patriarchy, this text demonstrates clearly that a woman can be a spiritual leader. Some interpreters claim God only did this because there was no male leader available. Nowhere does the text even remotely suggest that this was the case. In fact, Barak was a military leader who took his orders from Deborah (Judges 4:14). The simple truth is God chose Deborah to lead.

Huldah—Prophet to a Good King

Let's look now to a prophet named Huldah. Both Judah and Israel suffered a string of evil kings. One of Judah's most godly kings was Josiah. When godly Josiah needed a word from the Lord, he sent his priests to consult the woman prophet Huldah. Josiah could have consulted any number of male prophets. Jeremiah, for example, was a contemporary. Instead, he chose Huldah. Huldah was clearly a respected spiritual leader in Judah. We find Huldah's story in 2 Kings 22:14–16.

> So the priest Hilkiah, Ahikam, Achbor, Shaphan, and Asaiah went to the prophetess Huldah the wife of Shallum son of Tikvah, son of Harhas, keeper of the wardrobe; she resided in Jerusalem in the Second Quarter, where they consulted her. She declared to them, "Thus says the LORD, the God of Israel: Tell the man who sent you to me, Thus says the LORD, I will indeed bring disaster on this place and on its inhabitants—all the words of the book that the king of Judah has read."

Because of patriarchy, males predominate as leaders in virtually every time and place on earth, yet God still calls and equips women like Huldah to prophesy and to lead.

Anna—Prophet of Christ's Redemption

Let's jump ahead several hundred years to the time of Jesus. When Jesus' parents took him to the temple for dedication, two persons prophesied over him. One was Simeon. The other was Anna. Luke 2:36–38 describes the encounter with Anna.

> There was also a prophet, Anna, the daughter of Phanuel, of the tribe of Asher. She was of a great age, having lived with her husband seven years after her marriage, then as a widow to the age of eighty-four. She never left the temple but worshiped there with fasting and prayer night and day. At that moment she came, and began to praise God and to speak about the child to all who were looking for the redemption of Jerusalem.

I do not believe in chance or coincidence in God's inspired word. It was no accident that a woman prophesied over Jesus. God called and equipped this faithful and godly woman who served day and night at the temple. God gave this woman the privilege of prophesying over Jesus. Inspired by the Holy Spirit, she had something that God wanted said. Catherine Booth challenges, "Can any one explain wherein this exercise of Anna's differed from that of Simeon, recorded just before? It was in the same public place, the temple. It was during the same service. It was equally public, for she spake of Him to all who looked for redemption in Jerusalem" (1859:15).

Women Proclaiming the Good News

Miriam, Deborah, Huldah, and Anna are all named women leaders that God called, equipped, and used for divine purposes. There likely were others who have gone unnamed. Psalm 68:11 is an interesting passage. The King James Version translates the text as: "The LORD gave the word: great was the company of those that published *it*."

The New Revised Standard Version translates the text: "The Lord gives the command; great is the company of those who bore the tidings:" The NRSV includes the note "the company of women." With this note included the text would read, "The Lord gives the command; great is the company of women who bore the tidings." This translation is consistent with the Hebrew. Benjamin Titus Roberts, founder of the Free Methodist denomination, suggests, "We make of it a prediction that in the days spoken of in this psalm, when 'Ethiopia shall stretch out her hands unto God,' women were to preach the Gospel" (1891:57–58). Dr. Adam Clark writes of this verse, " 'Of the female preachers there was a great host.' Such is the literal translation of this passage...." (1825:432). God calls women to proclaim the good news. Considering the witness of Miriam, Deborah, Huldah, and Anna, God clearly calls and equips women to be prophets and spiritual leaders.

Jamal, you raised the question whether leadership in the Old Testament was a men's club. Because of the curse of sin, men have dominated virtually everywhere. God has, however, always called women to be prophets and leaders. Sinful human cultures do not encourage women to preach or lead. Sinful human cultures minimize what women have to say, even when they speak for God.

I pray one day that the whole church will renounce the sinful discrimination of patriarchy and accept the ministries of all who are called and equipped by God. God wants to speak through our Christian sisters. May God bless your congregation as you seek an associate pastor. If the best candidate is a woman, receive her with gratitude and follow her leadership.

In Christian love,

Randy

Discussion Questions for Chapter 3

1. Since some claim women cannot be leaders, why is it significant that the prophet Micah grouped Moses, Aaron, and Miriam together as persons "sent before the people"?

2. Some claim that God will not allow women to have authority over men. How does Deborah's lofty position as the spiritual, judicial, and military leader of Israel refute that claim?

3. If women are to keep silent what is the significance of one of Judah's most righteous kings seeking the counsel of a female prophet, Huldah?

4. If God doesn't allow women to prophesy or teach, why did God bless Anna with the privilege of prophesying over Jesus?

5. What evidence can you give that patriarchy is not God's intention for the human race?

6. How has the curse of sin affected women's roles in our society and around the world?

A Sexist Savior

Chapter 4

Dear Pastor Randy:

My name is Katrina Webber. I'm an eighteen year old high school senior. I have been raised in the church. All my life I've believed. Now I'm having tremendous doubts. My Sunday school teacher has been making many sexist statements about women's roles in the church, family, and society. His anti-woman comments have prompted me to study patriarchy. The more I read, the madder I get. There's no way that men should be in charge of everything. Women are more than sex objects. We are more than baby makers. We have spiritual gifts and brains. We have talents, hopes and dreams. My Sunday school teacher said women are supposed to always submit to men. It seems so unfair. I could handle it if my Sunday school teacher were the only one with these views but the whole church acts like they agree with him. I have many goals and plans. One day I'd like to get married and have children, but I also believe God wants me to be a medical doctor. I might even become a medical missionary. It would be great to care for the whole person, body, soul, and spirit. Lately, I have been wondering if any of it could ever happen.

I guess I might be able to accept that the church has been tainted by patriarchy but I can't bear to think that Jesus, my Savior, was sexist. Yet as I think about it, I don't know what else to think. My Sunday school teacher noted last week that Jesus called only male disciples. He only chose *men as apostles. He didn't include any women. I love the Gospel but I don't think I can serve a sexist God.*

Our church doesn't have a pastor right now. Our youth leader, Karl Heinrich, said you might be able to answer my questions. I don't want to forsake my faith. Please write back soon.

Sincerely,

Katrina Webber

Dear Katrina:

Thank you so much for trusting me with your questions and concerns. I hope that I will be able to help. I want to begin by affirming some things. First, cling to your faith. Your walk with God is the "pearl of great price." Nothing will ever bless you more than living for Jesus Christ. Jesus is life: abundant, eternal, and free. Over all my years, nothing has given me more satisfaction than loving and serving the Lord. Second, it excites me to see that you have godly goals and plans. I first heard God's call to be a pastor when I was twelve years old. It's wonderful to sense God's call in your life. God loves you and has gifted you with your temperament, gifts, and talents. God plans to bless and use you. Pursue God's call to be a doctor. Whether you serve at home or in another country, you can do much good. Third, I think it's great that you are asking questions about patriarchy. Many persons in the church simply accept patriarchy without ever really questioning its validity. I firmly believe that patriarchy is the curse of sin and not the plan of God. God created men and women to be equals. God made both in the divine image. God gave both dominion over the earth. There was no hierarchy at creation. Subjugation of women came with the fall. Praise God, Jesus sets us free from the curse of sin!

Jesus Valued and Respected Women

I hope that I can help you to understand that Jesus was not sexist. In fact, more than any other person of his time, Jesus valued and respected women. His attitude toward women was revolutionary and positively affects the treatment of women to this day.

Life for women in Jesus' time was anything but equal with men. Patriarchy was deeply entrenched and virtually every institution was deeply sexist. Rabbis wouldn't teach women the law. In the first century Rabbi Eliezer wrote,

"Rather should the words of the Torah be burned than entrusted to a woman ..." (*Mishnah Sotah* 3, 4) (Swidler, 1979:154). Women were not permitted to be priests. They had no place in the synagogue. They had limited property rights. They generally lived to serve their fathers and husbands. Women were largely relegated to domestic responsibilities and home related businesses. They could not freely converse with men on the streets. In the *Proverbs of the Fathers* we find the statement, "Speak not much with a woman" (*Mishnah Aboth* 1, 5) (Swidler,1979:156). This is a remarkable statement, especially when one considers that it was referring to men conversing with their own wives. "The rabbis generally assigned to women a very inferior place but there is no sign of this in the life and ministry of Jesus. On the contrary, he talked to women, cared for them, healed them, freely admitted them to fellowship and accepted their service" (Mary Evans, 1983:48).

Female Disciples of Jesus

Katrina, in your letter you wrote that Jesus called no female disciples. This may surprise you but Jesus actually traveled with women. Look at Luke 8:1–3.

> Soon afterwards he went on through cities and villages, proclaiming and bringing the good news of the kingdom of God. The twelve were with him, as well as some women who had been cured of evil spirits and infirmities: Mary, called Magdalene, from whom seven demons had gone out, and Joanna, the wife of Herod's steward Chuza, and Susanna, and many others, who provided for them out of their resources.

Luke specifically names three women and notes that there were "many" others. It was scandalous for Jesus to have female disciples but he taught them anyway. He loved them. He trusted them. They were partners in his ministry. They gave out of their own resources to keep the ministry thriving and growing. Joanna was married to the manager of King Herod's house. Like the male disciples Joanna and these "many" female disciples left their homes behind to travel and minister with Jesus.

Jesus' Friend Mary Chose the "Better Part"

Jesus' attitude was revolutionary when compared with other Jewish rabbis and leaders. "He went so far as to commend women as examples of faith and spiritual vitality, women who no rabbi would teach, women who were not counted in the number of a synagogue, who were isolated to a separate court at the temple, and whose religious vows could be overturned by their husbands" (S. C. Pearson, 1996:147). Jesus actually taught women and trusted them as friends. You remember the gospel accounts of Mary and Martha. The Gospels refer to Lazarus, Mary, and Martha as Jesus' friends. Look at Luke 10:38–42.

> Now as they went on their way, he entered a certain village, where a woman named Martha welcomed him into her home. She had a sister named Mary, who sat at the Lord's feet and listened to what he was saying. But Martha was distracted by her many tasks; so she came to him and asked, "Lord, do you not care that my sister has left me to do all the work by myself? Tell her then to help me." But the Lord answered her, "Martha, Martha, you are worried and distracted by many things; there is need of only one thing. Mary has chosen the better part, which will not be taken away from her."

The rabbis would not teach women. Rabbi Eliezer taught, "Whoever teaches his daughter the Torah is like one who teaches her obscenity" (*Mishnah Sotah* 3,4) (Swidler, 1979:154). Jesus gladly taught his friend, Mary. Cowles takes the evidence one step farther. Not only did Jesus teach Mary as he taught male disciples, he violated rabbinic tradition. And then "Jesus not only violated rabbinic tradition but offended Martha's sense of propriety when he permitted Mary to hear the Word. When Martha complained that Mary was not fulfilling her proper domestic role in the kitchen, he defended her: 'Mary has chosen the good part, which shall not be taken away from her' (Luke 10:42, NASB). In so doing, *Jesus affirmed the right of women to hear God's Word!*

"In his gentle rebuke, Jesus was stating a new principle that would break the autocracy of women's culturally and socially imposed role: namely, *it is more important for women to attend to the Word of God than it is to fulfill household duties.* A woman is greater than what she does. She has worth and dignity apart from childbearing" (1993:86).

Jesus Lived Far above the Sexist Patriarchy of His Time.

He was also no racist or legalist. Do you remember the account, found in John 4 of the Samaritan woman at the well? Jesus, tired from a journey through Samaria, sat down by Jacob's well and struck up a conversation with a Samaritan woman. The hatred between Jews and Samaritans ran deep for centuries. Jews and Samaritans did not associate with one another or drink from the same wells, yet Jesus did both. He was no racist. This woman was a known sinner who had to draw her water at noon because other respectable women wouldn't associate with her. In their conversation, Jesus noted that she had known five husbands and the man she was living with was not her husband. "Strike one": she was a Samaritan. "Strike two": she was a sinner. Respectable people don't associate with sinners. "Strike three": she was a woman. No self-respecting man would talk with such a woman in public. Jesus had an in-depth conversation with this precious soul. He was no racist. He was no legalist. He was no sexist.

In the course of their conversation, this woman recognized that Jesus was the promised Christ. Look at John 4:25–42.

> The woman said to him, "I know that Messiah is coming" (who is called Christ). "When he comes, he will proclaim all things to us." Jesus said to her, "I am he, the one who is speaking to you." Just then his disciples came. They were astonished that he was speaking with a woman, but no one said, "What do you want?" or, "Why are you speaking with her?" Then the woman left her water jar and went back to the city. She said to the people, "Come and see a man who told me everything I have ever done! ... Many Samaritans from that city believed in him because of the woman's testimony, "He told me everything I have ever done." So when the Samaritans came to him, they asked him to stay with them; and he stayed there two days. And many more believed because of his word. They said to the woman, "It is no longer because of what you said that we believe, for we have heard for ourselves, and we know that this is truly the Savior of the world."

The Woman at the Well—First to Proclaim the Messiah to the Samaritans

Katrina, some try to say that women shouldn't preach or teach. Jesus' attitude was totally different. Who was the first person in the Gospel of John to proclaim that Jesus is the Christ to the Samaritans? That first person was this woman. Our text says many Samaritans believed in Jesus because of her testimony. Clearly, the Holy Spirit used this woman for great good. Because of her ministry, Jesus stayed and ministered in partnership with this transformed woman for two days. Jesus acknowledged and partnered with this woman to win a spiritual harvest in Samaria. His ministry was possible because she preached the Christ to her people. Jesus values and respects the lives and ministries of women.

Jesus—A Savior Who Makes the Unclean Clean

Do you remember the story of the woman who had a bleeding problem? Her problems ran far deeper than bleeding. She was ceremonially unclean. To say that she was unclean was to say that she was ceremonially impure. The Hebrew is *Taw me* and means "not fit to enter the presence of God." One of the reasons that no women could be priests was that male priests feared being polluted by contact with menstruating women. Take a glance at Leviticus 15:19: "When a woman has a discharge of blood that is her regular discharge from her body, she shall be in her impurity for seven days, and whoever touches her shall be unclean until the evening." Leviticus 15:25 adds, "If a woman has a discharge of blood for many days, not at the time of her impurity, or if she has a discharge beyond the time of her impurity, all the days of the discharge she shall continue in uncleanness; as in the days of her impurity, she shall be unclean." Fearful of being contaminated, many men refused to teach women. They didn't want to risk being defiled.

Katrina, do you sense the tragedy in all this? At creation, God blessed women with the marvelous gift of bearing children. In the curse of sin following the fall, God predicted that women's pains in childbirth would increase. God's prediction became a sad reality. Because of the curse, a wonderful biological function became a vivid reminder of the fall. Women would be unclean during their menstruation. Patriarchy would ensure that males fearing defilement by menstruating women would keep women on the margins of society. Leviticus brims full of purity laws for men, women, and even animals. It grapples with the issues of holiness in an unholy world. The fall made a wide gulf between a holy God and creation. Jesus Christ bridged that gulf by his death and resurrection. Jesus brought reconciliation between our holy God and fallen humanity (2 Cor 5:17–19). The blood of Jesus Christ obliterates the curse of sin. Something wonderful happened in the encounter between Jesus and the bleeding woman. Jesus shattered the values of his day. Look at Matthew 9:20–22. "Then suddenly a woman who had been suffering from hemorrhages for twelve years came up behind him and touched the fringe of his cloak, for she said to herself, 'If I only touch his cloak, I will be made well.' Jesus turned, and seeing her he said, 'Take heart, daughter; your faith has made you well.' And instantly the woman was made well."

According to Leviticus, this woman was unclean. She was unfit to be in the presence of God. Anyone who came in contact with her would also be unclean. Did Jesus treat this bleeding woman as unclean? When she touched Jesus did he scold her and send her away? Did Jesus declare that she was unfit to be in his divine presence? Did Jesus himself become unclean? None of the above! Jesus welcomed this woman's touch. He then praised her faith and made her well. Jesus did not become unclean. By his touch he made her clean. When women touch Jesus with faith they become clean. The curse is gone! Jesus was no sexist. He loved, accepted, and healed women and by his touch has made them clean.

Jesus—No Double Standard Against Women

Jesus also showed mercy to the woman caught in adultery. The Jewish law commanded that when persons were caught in adultery both the man and the woman should be stoned to death (Lev 20:10). In John 8, the adulterous woman's accusers brought only the woman to Jesus. Jesus refused to apply a moral double standard against her. He refused to condemn her and left her with the directive to "sin no more."

> In all that we have heard and read against the right of a woman to be, in the fullest sense, a minister of the Gospel, we have never heard or read a single quotation for the words of Jesus against this right. This is significant. Christ applied the same rules of moral conduct to the woman as to the man. His treatment of the woman taken in adultery has scarcely a parallel. No woman who ever came to him was repulsed (Benjamin Titus Roberts, 1891:37).

Sharon Clark Pearson sums up the evidence. Jesus "…. challenged the sexist standards of his world—the lustful glance of an adulterous heart (Matt 5:27–28), the casual divorce, a male prerogative (Matt 19:3–9), and the threat of capital punishment applied unfairly—only to the adulterous woman (John 8:1–11)" (1996:147–148). There wasn't a sexist bone in Jesus' body.

Women—Last at the Cross, First to Proclaim the Gospel of the Resurrection

In the fullness of God's planning, God placed women center stage in the two most important events in the history of the world. Women were the last at the cross and the first at the tomb. All four gospels record the presence of women at Jesus' crucifixion (Matt 27:55–56, Mark 15:40–41, Luke 23:49, John 19:25–27). Matthew notes that there were "many women" present. "Many women were also there, looking on from a distance; they had followed Jesus from Galilee and had provided for him. Among them were Mary Magdalene, and Mary the mother of James and Joseph, and the mother of the sons of Zebedee" (Matt 27:55–56). Matthew, Mark, and Luke note that women were indeed last at the cross as they were present when Jesus' body was laid in the tomb (Matt 27:59–61, Mark 15:47, Luke 23:55–56). Jesus' female disciples and friends chose to be as faithful to him as he had been to them. All four gospels also record that women were the first to meet the resurrected Jesus at the tomb (Matt 28:1–10, Mark 16:1–9, Luke 24:1–10, John 20:1–18). Women were also the first to proclaim the gospel of the risen Lord. This was no accident. God could have given men this privilege. The first preachers of the resurrection were women. Cowles advances the argument: "After centuries of being denied access to the Word of God, and being locked out of full access to the worship of God in Temple and synagogue, it is almost as if God were saying, 'These are my beloved daughters, in whom I am well-pleased. Listen to them!'" (1993:95). Clearly God trusts women to proclaim the good news!

Only Male Apostles—A Weak Argument Against Female Leadership

Katrina, you noted that your Sunday school teacher indicated that Jesus chose only male apostles. He concluded from this that women cannot be leaders in the church. This is a weak argument. Jesus did not choose any Gentile apostles either. Should we conclude that only Jews can be apostles or church leaders? He only included Palestinian apostles, those in his own area. Should we conclude that all apostles and church leaders must be Palestinian? Deeply rooted patriarchy limited Jesus' options. Jesus sent only male apostles on preaching missions. What choice did he have? Women were denied education. They had no access to the Hebrew scriptures. They were not permitted to preach in the synagogues. Men would not give them a hearing in public forums. Women's testimony was not accepted in courts of law. Women had few rights in Jesus' day so expediency required that Jesus' earliest apostles be men. This does not mean that women cannot currently lead the church anymore than it means that all church leaders must be Palestinian Jews. Tragically, even today there are many who persist in marginalizing the spiritual gifts and contributions of God-called women. It is not that women are incapable. For centuries, patriarchal prejudices and misunderstandings such as this one have seriously hindered women's options.

Blessed Through Mary

Another indication that our Savior was not sexist was his treatment of his mother. God lifted Mary to a blessed state. Without the aid of any man, she bore in her womb the incarnate Son of God. No person in history can claim the unspeakable blessing that God granted to Mary. Look afresh at some of the marvelous words of the Magnificat:

> And Mary said, "My soul magnifies the Lord, and my spirit rejoices in God my Savior, for he has looked with favor on the lowliness of his servant. Surely, from now on all generations will call me blessed" (Luke 1:46–48).

Some have argued that all women are cursed through Eve. Why are not all women also blessed through Mary? "If all women are bound under Eve's curse, why then are not all released under Mary's blessing? How could we ever imagine that God would trust to a woman the birth, care, and nurture of His only begotten Son and yet deny her full freedom to proclaim the gospel of that very same Son?" (Cowles, 1993:82).

Katrina, from Jesus' treatment of his mother to every woman who crossed his path, Jesus ascribed to women respect and dignity far beyond any other prominent person of his time. Women ministered with Jesus and were integral to his life and ministry from before his birth, through his entire ministry, at the cross, and finally at the tomb. His open and sensitive treatment of women far exceeds even many from our own time. Rest assured. Jesus Christ is no sexist Savior! Jesus is in your court, cheering you on to faithfully fulfill your call. Continue to worship and serve your living, loving, and liberating Lord. May God greatly prosper your life and your ministry.

In Christian Love,

Pastor Randy

Discussion Questions for
Chapter 4

1. Why is it significant that Jesus taught women and that women traveled with him as disciples?

2. What is the importance of Jesus saying of Mary, as she was learning at his feet, that she had chosen the "better part"?

3. What importance can we place on the fact the first person to proclaim that Jesus is the Christ to the Samaritans was the woman at the well?

4. What conclusions might we draw from Jesus' encounter with the woman with the bleeding problem? Did Jesus become unclean or did she become clean?

5. What conclusions might we draw from Jesus' treatment of the woman caught in adultery?

6. What are the implications for women preachers that the very first persons to proclaim the gospel of Jesus' resurrection were women?

7. Why is the argument that Jesus chose only male apostles a weak argument against women in leadership?

8. What is the significance of the Virgin Mary's blessing for all believers?

PAUL SAYS

Chapter 5

Dear Pastor Huber:

My name is Irene Imbrone. You don't know me but your friend, Don Ortez, suggested that I contact you. He said you might be able to help. I'm in a bit of a tough place. I vowed that it would never happen, but somehow I got appointed onto our church pulpit committee. Frankly, I'm pretty uncomfortable. I'm one of two women on the committee. Our church chairperson said we needed some female input but I would rather that the men would choose our next pastor. My discomfort is bad enough being a woman on a committee that should just be men, but now our committee is considering calling a woman pastor. I'm mortified! I have studied the Bible all of my life and the Apostle Paul is absolutely clear about women having authority in the church. In 1 Corinthians 14:33–36 Paul says, "… for God is a God not of disorder but of peace. (As in all the churches of the saints, women should be silent in the churches. For they are not permitted to speak, but should be subordinate, as the law also says. If there is anything they desire to know, let them ask their husbands at home. For it is shameful for a woman to speak in church. Or did the word of God originate with you? Or are you the only ones it has reached?)." How could that be any more plain? I also refer to 1 Timothy 2:11–12. Paul says, "Let a woman learn in silence with full submission. I permit no woman to teach or to have authority over a man; she is to keep silent."

I am considering resigning my position on the pulpit committee and maybe even leaving the church. I really don't want to leave because I have attended here for years but I don't know what else to do. Don said maybe you could help. Please get back to me soon. Thank you.

Your Christian Sister,

Irene Imbrone

Dear Irene,

I certainly appreciate your discomfort in this situation. Many Christians believe exactly as you do about the Apostle Paul's position on women ministers. They affirm that Paul is absolutely opposed to women preachers and leaders in the church. They invariably quote the precise verses that you quoted. I don't know how you were raised or where you picked up your knowledge of the Bible, but for many years I believed much as you do. What I am about to write might make you a bit uncomfortable. I was uneasy when I began exploring this issue. Hang in there with me. I am about to suggest that the belief that you are expressing—and that I once held—is an unfortunate and common error. I can tell from your letter that you believe the Bible, so it is to the Bible that I will appeal. Like you, I am also firmly committed to God's word. I won't begin with the verses with which you started. We'll deal with them later.

Galatians 3:28 Proclaims the Biblical Equality of Men and Women

I want to begin with Paul's teaching in Galatians 3:28. Most Bible scholars believe that Galatians is the earliest of Paul's letters. This verse is one of the core principles of Paul's theology. Galatians 3:28 says, "There is no longer Jew or Greek, there is no longer slave or free, there is no longer male and female; for all of you are one in Christ Jesus." What is this verse saying? It is not saying there are no differences between Jews and Greeks, slaves or free or male and female. There clearly are differences. Paul is saying that in the church there should be no distinctions made between Jews and Greeks, slaves and free, male and female. All are saved by the same Savior. All are baptized with the same Spirit. All are empowered for the same ministry. No believer should discriminate against a Greek, a slave, or a woman. This text has been extremely important in American history. It helped to abolish slavery and to win women the right to vote. "Galatians 3:28 became the Magna Carta text for

Evangelicals advocating the abolition of slavery, as well as the enfranchisement of women" (Cowles, 1993:116). It is a prominent and important text for biblical equality.

Some conservative scholars, such as Alexander Strauch, argue that this text refers only to salvation. Jesus Christ equally saves Jews and Greeks, slaves and free, males and females. This narrow interpretation misses the full impact of the text. Not only does Jesus save us but Jesus also transforms and empowers us. Through Christ, we become members of the church and coheirs with Christ. Paul spent much of his ministry arguing for the inclusion of Gentiles in the church. He labored extensively to ensure that Gentiles became leaders and full participants at every level. He also wrote to Philemon appealing for him to accept the runaway slave, Onesimus, as a brother in the Lord. He also labored side by side with several prominent women leaders. Susie Stanley concludes, "Contrary to some arguments, we do have evidence that male/female equality was implemented in the New Testament era" (Mickelsen, 1986:182). Paul put Galatians 3:28 into practice. It truly is his Magna Carta of equality. In the nineteenth century, Benjamin Titus Roberts argued for the church to accept women as pastors. Appealing to Galatians 3:28, he wrote of women, "Under the blessed spirit of Christianity they have equal rights, equal privileges, and equal blessings, and, let me add, they are equally useful" (1891:40). Roberts drew these conclusions by observing how vigorously Paul applied his instructions in Galatians 3:28 in his life.

Paul Respected and Valued the Leadership Ministries of Women

Romans chapter 16 clearly demonstrates this point. The Book of Romans is nearly universally acclaimed as Paul's most complete theological argument. We see in Romans Paul's fullest explanation of the gospel and, from the twelfth chapter on, practical instructions for the church. In chapter 16, Paul concludes the letter with greetings to numerous important persons. Ten of those important persons are women. These women are Phoebe, Priscilla, Mary, Junia, Tryphena, Tryphosa, Persis, Rufus' mother, Julia, and Nereus' sister. This impressive list demonstrates how completely Paul respected the leadership of women in the church.

Phoebe—Deacon in the Church

The very first person mentioned is Phoebe. Romans 16:1–2 says, "I commend to you our sister Phoebe, a deacon of the church at Cenchreae, so that you may welcome her in the Lord as is fitting for the saints, and help her in whatever she may require from you, for she has been a benefactor of many and of myself as well." Phoebe is a deacon, a leader. This same word, *diakonos,* is used to describe prominent men with leadership standing in the church (1 Tim 3:8–12).

> When referring to Phoebe, however, most translators reveal their traditionalist bias by rendering diakonos as "servant" or "deaconess" because they cannot imagine a woman as a "minister." This translation lacks integrity and should not be the case. Diakonos appears in both masculine and feminine cases in the Greek, depending upon the gender of the one it modifies. In this instance, however, the rule is broken. Diakonos is masculine, even though it refers to a woman. It seems clear that Paul wants to communicate that Phoebe is more than someone who waits on tables. Neither is she a "deaconess," but just as much a full and respected minister of the Word as, for instance, Timothy or Titus, or even Paul himself (Cowles, 1993:101).

This understanding is reinforced by Paul's instructions that the leaders of the church should "welcome" Phoebe and seek to "help her in whatever she may require from you." This instruction makes sense only if Phoebe is a minister like her male counterparts.

Priscilla—Prominent Teacher and Leader in the Church

Priscilla also was a prominent leader in the church. When the great orator, Apollos, needed to be taught, Priscilla and Aquila took the challenge.

> Now there came to Ephesus a Jew named Apollos, a native of Alexandria. He was an eloquent man, well versed in the scriptures. He had been instructed in the Way of the Lord; and he spoke with burning enthusiasm and taught accurately the things concerning Jesus, though he knew only the baptism of John. He began to speak boldly in the synagogue; but when Priscilla and Aquila heard him, they took him aside and explained the Way of God to him more accurately (Acts 18:24–26).

Priscilla, a woman, actually took the lead in teaching Apollos, an educated and eloquent man. She is named first in Acts 18. She is also named first in Romans 16. Priscilla and Aquila were a husband and wife team. In a patriarchal culture it is amazing that Priscilla is mentioned by name at all. Even more remarkable is that when Priscilla is named, sometimes she is named before her husband. Word order is an important component in Greek grammar. The fact that Priscilla is mentioned first implies that she was a stronger leader than her husband. Amazingly, in a patriarchal culture that kept women in subjection, in four of the six places in the New Testament where Priscilla and Aquila are mentioned, Priscilla is named first (Acts 18:18, Acts 18:26, Rom 16:3, 2 Tim 4:19). Also, "By calling Priscilla a fellow worker in Christ Jesus, the Apostle Paul accorded Priscilla an equal place among other such workers as Timothy (Rom 16:21), Titus (2 Cor 8:23), Luke (Philem 24), Apollos, Paul (1 Cor 3:9), and others" (S. C. Pearson, 1996:149). She clearly was a valued teacher and leader and "fellow worker" with Paul in the church.

Junia—A Female Apostle

Next we need to consider Junia in Romans 16:7. Paul writes, "Greet Andronicus and Junia, my relatives who were in prison with me; they are prominent among the apostles, and they were in Christ before I was." Some Bibles, such as the New International Version, the New English Bible, the New American Standard translate what is a female name in Greek, "Junia," as the male name, "Junias." This translation may reflect male translator's bias. *Junia* was a common female name in Paul's day but there is no credible record of any male name "Junias." If we acknowledge that the proper translation is Junia, then we must conclude that Junia was a female apostle. Apostleship was the highest respected position in the early church. As Booth notes, even the influential fourth-century church father, John Chrysostom, not known a supporter of women, believed that Junia was a woman (1859:11). Other early church leaders, Origen of Alexandria (185–233 AD) and Jerome (340–420 AD) accepted Junia as a woman apostle and then "apparently no commentator until Aegidius of Rome (1245–1316 AD) took the name to be masculine" (Bonnie Thurston, 1998:57). The best evidence is clearly that Junia was a female apostle.

Euodia and Syntyche—Paul's Co-workers in the Gospel

In Paul's letter to the Philippians, he urges two prominent female leaders in the church to "work together." Look at Philippians 4:2–3. "I urge Euodia and I urge Syntyche to be of the same mind in the Lord. Yes, and I ask you also, my loyal companion, help these women, for they have struggled beside me in the work of the gospel, together with Clement and the rest of my co-workers, whose names are in the book of life." Paul describes Euodia and Syntyche as women who have "struggled beside me in the gospel." Paul urges his "loyal companion" to help these women. It's unlikely that Paul is asking key leaders in the church to help wash dishes or make beds. Paul calls these women his "co-workers" in "the work of the gospel" worthy of the help of other leaders in the church.

Phillip's Four Preaching Daughters

Irene, I hope that you can see that Paul consistently practiced the principles of biblical equality found in Galatians 3:28. He constantly affirmed the leadership of women in his ministry. When Paul was traveling he stayed at the house of Philip the evangelist. Paul accepted the ministry of Philip's daughters who were prophets. Prophets are those who proclaim the word of God. "The next day we left and came to Caesarea; and we went into the house of Philip the evangelist, one of the seven, and stayed with him. He had four unmarried daughters who had the gift of prophecy" (Acts 21:8–9).

Churches Meeting in the Homes of Female Church Leaders

Paul also accepted the leadership of women when they offered their homes as meeting places for emerging churches. The first church in Asia met at Lydia's home. Rosalind Miles notes:

> Indeed the very first Christian churches in Rome and elsewhere were houses donated by wealthy widows, and all the Christian communities in Acts of the Apostles are recorded as meeting under a woman's roof: 'the church in the house of Chloe, in the house of Lydia, in the house of Mary, the mother of Mark, in the house of Nympha, in the house of Prisca …'" (2001:86).

Chloe—Leader of a Church Delegation

Paul acknowledged the leadership and spiritual gifts of other women. Paul wrote his letter, First Corinthians, at least in part, as a response to the concerns of a woman named Chloe. "For it has been reported to me by Chloe's people that there are quarrels among you, my brothers and sisters" (1 Cor 1:11). It is significant that Paul respected Chloe and the people she sent to keep him informed. Chloe was likely a wealthy and respected business-person. Paul trusted Chloe and her "people."

Public Prayer and Preaching of Women in Corinth

In Corinth, Paul also acknowledged the rights of women to pray and prophesy in a public service of worship. Paul deals with problems in worship services at Corinth in 1 Corinthians, chapters 11—14, specifically in 1 Corinthians 11:3–16.

Paul clearly allows women to pray and prophesy during worship. "But any woman who prays or prophesies with her head unveiled disgraces her head—it is one and the same thing as having her head shaved" (1 Cor 11:5). To prophesy is to speak God's Word. The most common expression of prophecy is "anointed preaching." It is clear in this text that Paul is not prohibiting women from praying and prophesying. His concern is the wearing of veils. Evans notes that, "These verses make it clear that while Paul is arguing in favour of differing customs for men and women regarding headgear, he takes it for granted that their behaviour in relation to prayer and prophecy will be parallel" (1983:86). The overarching concern in this whole section of 1 Corinthians is decency and order in worship. Richard Longenecker concludes, "So it was not a question of women praying or prophesying in the congregation, but rather the manner in which they did so" (Mickelsen, 1985:72). In Corinth, Paul taught that women should not pray or preach with their heads uncovered.

Most churches today no longer concern themselves with the issue of veils. Veils are rightly viewed as an accommodation to culture in Paul's day. For married women in the Greco-Roman world of Paul's day to refuse to wear veils was roughly analogous to married women refusing to wear their wedding rings today. In the great cities of the Grecian world, only prostitutes did not wear veils. It was scandalous and upsetting to the status quo for godly women to dress like prostitutes. It was a shame to the husbands, the church, and to the gospel. For women to preach while violating these obvious social customs was an unnecessary distraction to the spread of the gospel. Never at issue in this text is the right of women to pray and prophesy in the church. Walter L. Liefield writes, "Paul thus is affirming that women do have the God-given right to pray and prophesy (Acts 2: 17) but that they can exercise that right only if they do so without causing social offense by bringing shame to their husbands through uncovered heads" (Mickelsen, 1985:146).

Some misuse this text to put great restrictions upon women in the church. This is violating the sense and context of the text. "Whatever Paul's statement does mean, it in no way functions in this text to limit the participation or leadership of women in public worship" (Pearson, 1996:152). Paul is requiring women to be sensitive to their social context while they are praying and prophesying in the congregation. He is concerned especially that they do not cause "disorder" through culturally inappropriate dress and behavior.

No Universal Intention of Silence for Either Men or Women

Irene, I now want to address the first text that you quoted in your letter, 1 Corinthians 14:33–36:

> ... for God is a God not of disorder but of peace. (As in all the churches of the saints, women should be silent in the churches. For they are not permitted to speak, but should be subordinate, as the law also says. If there is anything they desire to know, let them ask their husbands at home. For it is shameful for a woman to speak in church. Or did the word of God originate with you? Or are you the only ones it has reached?).

As I have already shown, Paul continually affirmed and valued the speaking ministries of women. As I just noted, three chapters earlier in this same letter, Paul allowed women to pray and prophesy in public. Whatever "silence" means in these verses clearly cannot disqualify all women for all time from using their spiritual gifts in the church. "No matter what final conclusion one places upon the instruction *to be silent,* it cannot be that women are not allowed to *pray or prophesy* in public worship" (Pearson, 1996: 153). Evans writes, "The majority of modern scholars take the view that what Paul requires is not total silence, but the limitation of some particular form of participation" (1983:97). Actually, Paul is specifically instructing Corinthian wives not to disrupt the worship services with inappropriate conversation. When you look at the original Greek, verse 34 reads literally "the women in the churches".... The definite article in the Greek indicates that Paul is addressing a specific group of women. This group was disruptive wives. This kind of instruction to married women was appropriate in Greek culture. Most married women had few opportunities for social interaction. They spent the bulk of their time shut up in their homes. They were not educated in spiritual matters. When these formerly house-bound married women found the new freedom to participate in worship in Christian community, even among men, their temptation to talk was great. These unschooled Corinthian wives had many questions and much to learn. Paul instructed them to take their questions to their husbands when they get home. This text in no way limits called and equipped women from exercising their spiritual gifts. It limits disruptive speech during worship. In an attempt to maintain *order* in the Corinthian worship, Paul set guidelines for Corinthian wives to worship in the Christian community without bringing confusion. He spoke of silence.

Paul could have selected several words for "silence." He used *sigao* which implies a voluntary silence. In Mark 14:61 it is the word used to describe Jesus' silence before Pilate. It is the same word that Paul addressed to men in 1 Corinthians 14:28 when he wrote "let him keep silent in the church" (NASB). If we take both commands for silence out of context, we have a church of silent women and men. Scriptural texts must be interpreted in their contexts. There are times for men and women to speak and there are times for men and women to be silent. Paul issued a double command not to speak in verses 34 and 35. The Greek word here translated as "speak" is *laleo*. Of all the Greek verbs translated as "speak," only *laleo* can mean simply "talk" or "chatter." Paul was not prohibiting all women for all time from teaching, praying, or preaching. Paul was prohibiting specific Corinthian wives from noisy, distracting conversation that was disrupting worship. Cowles usefully summarizes the issues for Corinthian wives in 1 Corinthians 11 and 14:

> However, for the sake of an ordered church service, restrain yourselves from undue exhibitionism in the exercise of spiritual gifts. Avoid idle conversation once the service has begun, and hold your questions until you can discuss them fully in the privacy of your home with your husband. Be careful to observe accepted social convention in dress and personal decorum in church in order that all may worship in a proper manner and that no unnecessary offense come upon the gospel (11:5–10) (1993:137).

No Absolute Prohibition Against Women Teaching and Exercising Authority

Now let's turn our attention to the other passage you quoted 1 Timothy 2:11–12. This is the most common text used to oppose women in ministry.

"Let a woman learn in silence with full submission. I permit no woman to teach or to have authority over a man; she is to keep silent." We could write a whole book just on this passage. It is quite a difficult text to interpret because of several contextual issues. Alan Padget identifies "... two approaches to 1 Timothy 2 concerning women; an absolutist reading that applies it to all times and places, and a contingent reading that finds the passage speaks to its original context, but which its author did not mean to be universal" (N.D.:24). Irene, I first want to show the problems with the absolutist viewpoint, then I want to explain the passage within its context.

I see six major problems with viewing this text as an absolute prohibition against women pastors in all times and places. First, this understanding clearly contradicts Paul's teachings and practices in the rest of the New Testament. As I have been demonstrating, Paul consistently practiced the biblical equality he puts forth in Galatians 3:28. "There is no longer Jew or Greek, there is no longer slave or free, there is no longer male and female; for all of you are one in Christ Jesus." He valued the leadership ministries of many women including, Priscilla, Lydia, Phoebe, Chloe, Junia, Euodia, Syntyche, Tryphena, Tryphosa, Persis, Rufus' mother, Julia, Nereus' sister and others. He allowed women to pray and prophecy in public worship at Corinth.

A second problem with reading this text as an absolute is that it contradicts Jesus' practices concerning women. His family accepted the prophetic ministry of Anna. Jesus affirmed the ministry of the woman at the well who was the first person in the Gospel of John to proclaim that Jesus is the Messiah to the Samaritans. All four gospels affirm that God gave to women the blessing of being the first to proclaim the gospel of the risen Lord.

Third, this absolutist understanding clearly violates God's practice of calling women into authority in the Old Testament. If the prohibition against women teaching or having authority over men is universal, how do we explain God calling Miriam, Deborah, Huldah, and Anna as prophetic leaders who spoke the word of God with authority?

Fourth, most of those who put forth this absolutist viewpoint are inconsistent in applying their absolutist principle on other issues in the very same chapter. Let's look at a few examples. "I desire, then, that in every place the men should pray, lifting up holy hands without anger or argument; also that the women should dress themselves modestly and decently in suitable clothing, not with their hair braided, or with gold, pearls, or expensive clothes, but with good works, as is proper for women who profess reverence for God" (1 Tim 2:8–10). Should we conclude from this text that "in every place" when men pray, they should pray only with their hands lifted up? Is having the hands lifted up the only option for men when they pray? I don't know a single credible scholar who would take this absolutist position. Or consider the issue of the appropriate dress for women. Is Paul saying that braided hair is absolutely and inherently inappropriate for godly females in all places and in all times? In our society, braided hair is considered a cute, modest, and decent hairstyle even for young children. In Ephesus, braided hair was considered sensuous. Conscientious biblical scholars must ask the question—which teachings are "particular" to a culture and which are universal, that is, for all people for all times?

Consider also how those who universalize that women cannot teach or have authority over men take the precise opposite approach when considering the childbirth issue later in our text. Look at 1 Timothy 2:15; "Yet she will be saved through childbearing, provided they continue in faith and love and holiness, with modesty." Is Paul teaching a new doctrine of salvation: women can be saved through childbearing or only through childbearing? If one universalizes that women cannot teach or have authority over men, why not also universalize that women can be saved through childbearing? You know from reading the New Testament that good works can save no one. For example, Ephesians 2:8–9 affirms, "For by grace you have been saved through faith, and this is not your own doing; it is the gift of God—not the result of works, so that no one may boast." Absolutist scholars, immersed in patriarchy, insist that women cannot be teachers or have authority over men with clear disregard for all of the other biblical texts that teach otherwise. But when considering salvation through childbirth, they cling to biblical texts that affirm salvation by faith and rightly refuse to universalize that women can be saved through childbirth. Why in the same passage is a prohibition about women teaching considered universal while salvation through childbirth is particular? Their exegetical methods are clearly arbitrary and inconsistent.

Fifth, an absolutist understanding is rooted in a rigid and narrow understanding of a very rare Greek verb. The verb that is commonly translated as "have authority" over a man is *authentein*. This verb is used only once in the entire New Testament, and that is in this text. It is highly speculative to translate a verb that is used only once in the New Testament, yet those who take a gender-based view of leadership base their *primary* biblical case against women in ministry on this one verse and one obscure verb. This verb has several meanings in the secular literature of Paul's day. Some examples are: "to act independently," "to dominate," "to exercise one's own judgment," and even "to commit murder." One definition offered by Catherine and Richard Kroeger is "author of" (1992:103). A more common rendering is "usurp authority." First Timothy 2:12 would translate, then, "I do not permit a woman to teach nor usurp authority over a man." Rev. Dr. Taft says, "This passage should be rendered 'I suffer not a woman to teach by usurping authority over the man'" (Booth, 1859:13).

Sixth, even those who take an absolutist position on this text and on 1 Corinthians 14 do not apply these passages literally. They often argue that women can pray in public. They can lead worship. They can testify. They can teach children. They can teach other women. They can write. They can prophesy, but they can't pastor a church. Taken universally, this text says nothing about pastoring a church. It prohibits women from teaching and requires their silence. Benjamin Titus Roberts notes:

> No denomination applies these passages literally. If they did, they would not allow:
> Women to sing in church. For to sing is not to keep silence.
> Nor to pray; for the same reason.
> Nor to testify; for to testify is to speak.
> Nor to teach in the Sabbath school or elsewhere; for the statement is general—I suffer not a woman to teach.
> Nor to write religious books, or for religious periodicals for this is to teach (1891:40–41).

Isn't it odd that those who claim to take this text literally don't actually take it literally? They claim that it prohibits women from being pastors but if they take it universally and absolutely, women cannot teach anyone of any age and cannot even speak. Clearly, the passage should not be interpreted as absolute.

Understanding 1 Timothy 2:11–12

Irene, as you can see, there are serious problems with taking an absolutist stand on 1 Timothy 2:11–12. How then should we properly interpret these verses? There are many helpful approaches. Here is my view, shared by others. First Timothy was written to the church at Ephesus. Sharon Clark Pearson writes, "All in all, the difficulties of this passage in 1 Timothy are best explained when the instruction is recognized as correction of false teaching and teachers at Ephesus" (1996:160). Ephesus was a center of goddess worship. It housed the temple of Artemis who is also called Diana. Ephesus was a city with considerable ambiguity toward women. Like most other places, women were at the bottom of the social ladder, yet ironically the Ephesians also worshiped female goddesses. Ephesus was also a center of proto-gnosticism. The early gnostic teachers were threatening the purity of the gospel. Such teachers sought secret knowledge and followed bizarre rituals. Catherine and Richard Kroeger do an excellent job of describing the Ephesian context in their book *I Suffer Not a Woman: Rethinking 1 Timothy 2:11–15 in Light of Ancient Evidence.* According to the Kroegers, some of these early gnostics taught that the woman was created first and then the man. They believed woman was thus the source of man (1992:105–113). This was one of many false teachings threatening the gospel at Ephesus. Paul encouraged the Ephesian church to vigorously combat false teachers (1 Timothy 1:3–7). The integrity of the gospel was at stake. Evans wrote, "1 Timothy 1:7 tells us that there were those in the church at Ephesus who wanted to be teachers but who did not have the necessary understanding and who went about it in quite the wrong way. It seems likely that some of the women formed part of this group and Paul was insisting that they must gain understanding before they can impart it" (1983:103). In this overall context, Paul was very sensitive to women usurping authority over a man or being domineering over him. He put special restrictions upon certain women at Ephesus to protect the integrity of the gospel in a hostile environment. Alan G. Padgett writes, "Paul's concern is that a quarrelsome church must not rock the boat during a time of persecution. He is not concerned to give universal marching orders for all time" (N.D.:27).

With this background, how might we interpret our text? "First of all, then, I urge that supplications, prayers, intercessions, and thanksgivings be made for everyone, for kings and all who are in high positions, so that we may lead a quiet and peaceable life in all godliness and dignity. This is right and is acceptable in the sight of God our Savior" (1 Tim 2:1–3). Paul's main concern is that the church live at peace in the larger society. The gospel of Jesus Christ is radical, but Paul did not want the Ephesian Christians to make waves. They did not need more riots in Ephesus like those that took place earlier (Acts 19). They were to pray for their leaders and "lead a quiet and peaceable life in all godliness and dignity." In this context Paul writes, "I desire, then, that in every place the men should pray, lifting up holy hands without anger or argument; also that the women should dress themselves modestly and decently in suitable clothing, not with their hair braided, or with gold, pearls, or expensive clothes, but with good works, as is proper for women who profess reverence for God" (1 Tim 2:8–9). Men are to be persons of peaceful prayer. Women are to be reverent and godly. They should not dress like the prostitutes in their city. They must not draw inappropriate attention to themselves.

We continue, "Let a woman learn in silence with full submission. I permit no woman to teach or to have authority over a man; she is to keep silent" (1 Tim 2:11–12). These women who needed to learn were likely new converts who did not yet understand the full implications of their faith. They were to quietly learn about the faith before they attempted to teach. Note the text does not say that their learning should be in submission "to men"; Padgett notes, "Rather, he simply tells them to learn in submission, that is in submission to sound teaching—not to men" (N.D.:27). With this context in mind, I paraphrase verse 12: "I permit no unprepared woman to teach or usurp authority over a man. Such an unprepared, unlearned person should keep silent."

Let's follow up with the last part of the text. Here Paul refers to Genesis. "For Adam was formed first, then Eve; and Adam was not deceived, but the woman was deceived and became a transgressor. Yet she will be saved through childbearing, provided they continue in faith and love and holiness, with modesty" (1 Tim 2:13–15). Paul is here combating a specific gnostic false teaching that was highly attractive to new female converts in a city that honored the goddess Diana. As I mentioned earlier, certain gnostic false teachers taught that woman was created first and was thus the source of the man. Paul corrects this mistaken notion. Women should not take license on the basis of a Gnostic false teaching to usurp authority over men. Catherine Kroeger notes another Gnostic heresy, that truly spiritual women would not bear children. To bear children was to be unacceptable to God (1992:172–177). Paul corrects this notion. Women will be saved even though they bear children as long "they continue in faith and love and holiness, with modesty."

Irene, this text addresses a very specific local situation in Ephesus. It limits certain ill-prepared women in a particular place and time from usurping authority. Paul could not have intended it as a universal teaching for all women in all places and times. He valued the teaching and preaching of women and did not attempt to prohibit women from being leaders in the church. Paul consistently affirmed the leadership of women. He constantly practiced Galatians 3:28: "There is no longer Jew or Greek, there is no longer slave or free, there is no longer male and female; for all of you are one in Christ

Jesus." It took the entire first century for the church to resolve the discrimination issues between Jews and Greeks. The distinctions between slave and free continue to be a problem all over the world. In the United States we did not end slavery until late in the nineteenth century and we still struggle with its horrible scars. The church is still struggling with the male and female issue. Some church leaders are still vigorous in keeping women from using their God given gifts in ministry.

I hope that you remain in your church and on the pulpit committee. You love God and the Bible. You have gifts and experience. Use your gifts and perspective to help your pulpit committee find the best possible pastor. If the person God wants to lead your church is a woman, help others to understand what I have shown you. Welcome her. Embrace her. Support her. Pray for her. The Apostle Paul would do no less.

May God bless you and your congregation with a wonderful pastor. Let me know how everything works out.

In Christian Love,

Pastor Randy

Discussion Questions for Chapter 5

1. What are the implications of Galatians 3:28 for women serving as leaders in the church?

2. How does the fact that Paul respected women leaders in the church refute the notion that Paul universally prohibits women from having authority in the church?

3. How does the fact that Paul permitted women to pray and prophesy in Corinth refute the idea that women must be universally silent in the church?

4. What arguments can you give that the statements of Paul in 1 Timothy 2:11–12 concerning women teaching, having authority and being silent are intended for a particular group of women in a particular place and time and are not intended to be universally applied to all women everywhere and for all time?

5. Why do you think some Bible interpreters, despite strong biblical evidence to the contrary, cling tenaciously to interpreting 1 Timothy 2:11–12 as universally prohibiting women from being pastors?

I'm a Stay-at-Home Mom
Chapter 6

Dear Pastor Randy,

    I really appreciate your ministry but I'm having a hard time understanding this women in ministry issue. You know me. I'm a stay-at-home mom. I adore my husband, Mark. I love all four of our children. I'm so grateful that my mom stayed home to raise my sisters and me. My father was a good provider. I came from a great home and I want my children to be raised in the same kind of home. I value Mark's headship. I appreciate the covering he gives to me. He's a wonderful husband and I want to submit to him. I want our children to be obedient. I want a biblical family.

    I'm convinced that a woman's place is in the home. I believe God has ordained that women stay home and take care of their husbands and children. "The hand that rocks the cradle is the hand that rules the world." Because of divorce or family financial problems some women must work but it's not what God wants. The traditional family is disappearing. There are so many single parent homes and latchkey kids. Kids need both parents. When both parents work, children are left without care. It's so sad!

    I believe that women aren't being taught the right things anymore. Women are going off working without a male covering. I know a few people who have had affairs at work. It's not healthy for men and women to work together. There are so many temptations.

    Women don't need to be pastors. They need to be wives and mothers.

Please don't be offended by what I'm writing. I just want you to understand how I feel. Women need to be at home. Thanks for your faithful ministry.

I'm God's child,

Janet

Dear Janet,

Thank you so much for sharing your feelings with me. I appreciate your faithfulness to God and the church. You and Mark are doing a great job raising your children. They are polite and show growing spiritual insight and passion. You have chosen to stay home with your family. I applaud that decision. You are a first-class person, a first-class Christian, and a first-class mom. I have great respect for every godly woman who seeks to be a good mother.

You might already know this, but we share similar family backgrounds. I also was raised in a traditional, middle class, white family. I grew up in Michigan and Indiana. My dad went to work and my mother stayed home and took care of the house, my sister, my brother, and me. I have good memories of my mom being around. I always felt secure knowing that mom was nearby. You also know that as soon as our oldest son Michael arrived, Susan gave up her career as an early childhood educator to be a stay-at-home mom. Susan has not worked outside of the home for seventeen years except for three years she served as a part-time tutor for a blind child. She has kept our family going. I appreciate that my mother and my wife, Susan, have had the opportunity to be stay-at-home moms. That is what they wanted to be. Like you, my mom and Susan have voluntarily chosen to stay home to serve their families.

Is Being a Stay-at-Home Mom a Woman's Only Function?

I think it is wonderful that my mom, Susan, and you have been stay-at-home moms. That was your choice. But is there room for women to choose to exercise their spiritual gifts outside of the home? Georgia Harkness wrote:

> God intends for women to continue to be partners with men in the propagation of the race. But it is a far cry from this deduction to say that this is the only function a woman has, or that all women ought to bear children or that a

child-bearing woman ought to continue on in this pursuit beyond reasonable limits of her own strength, of the father's economic situation, or the well being of the children already born and needing the family's care and resources" (1972:187–88).

I believe that women should be allowed to pursue options. This is especially true when they are called by God to do ministry. Edward C. Lehman wrote, "One source of attitudes toward clergywomen is attitudes toward women's roles in general. Religious sexism is in many ways but an extension of secular sexism" (1987:322). Women should not be locked in to domestic responsibilities only. Women should be allowed to pursue their interests and spiritual gifts. Even in the nineteenth century, Wesleyan/holiness women came to realize that God's call could extend beyond the domestic sphere. Susie Stanley summarizes her historical research by writing: "The confining boundaries of women's sphere could not contain Wesleyan/Holiness women preachers who appealed to a higher authority to break through the invisible barriers intended to inhibit their activities" (2002:22). She adds, "Rather than accepting the argument that motherhood precluded the possibility of preaching, women accepted their responsibilities as mothers but contended that the sanctified self gave priority to God's work" (2002:126). God calls many women to be mothers, but God also calls women to many other important responsibilities. I support women doctors, women business owners, and women pastors. If men can be pastors and still be husbands and fathers, why can't women be pastors and still be wives and mothers?

Some Childcare Options for Women Pastors

You mentioned latchkey kids. I am also saddened that children are left without proper supervision and care. Children are treasures. As parents we need to provide excellent and continual care and protection for our children. Are stay-at-home mothers the only ones who can do a quality job? I know many excellent mothers who have careers outside of the home. I also believe that dads have an equal responsibility in raising children. When a mother supervises her children, we say that she is being a "mom." When a father supervises his children, we commonly say that he is "babysitting." Why don't we say that he is being a "dad"? Sadly, many men don't spend near enough time raising their children. We men need to do our part in order to allow called women to use their spiritual gifts. Dads can make it possible for moms to be pastors or serve the Lord in other ways by doing their full share of work around the house and in the family.

There are other excellent ways for female pastors to provide safe and loving child care. Some families are blessed to have extended family nearby. Some communities have outstanding day care. Some congregations provide excellent childcare. Some women pastors have a working understanding with other families in the church. They can drop their children off at any time at a moment's notice for an emergency or crisis. All of these options enable women both to be excellent pastors and excellent mothers.

Even employers can be of assistance in enhancing parenting. Employers can provide flex-time. Moms and dads can arrange their schedules so that the children are always with either mom or dad. One of the most ideal arrangements is co-pastoring. Husband and wife teams equally share leadership in the church and responsibilities at home. The church is blessed by having two dedicated leaders. The children are blessed by having quality time with both of their parents. I wish my parents could have done something like that. I saw a lot of my mom, who was always home, but my dad had to work long hours out of the house. I didn't get near as much time with him. It would have been great if I could have spent more time with dad.

Employers can also allow work to be done from the home. This is especially practical for pastors. At Chapel Hill Church of God, Pastor Mike LeMay and I both have our church offices in our homes. This enables us to be more available for our families. Frequently, Pastor LeMay works in his living room so that he can keep an eye on his adorable infant son, Nathan. Many times I have done my church work with my children in my office. They have watched television, played on the floor, and done their homework. We have had great times together even as I have been working. As I type this letter, Susan is sitting here in my office reading today's mail. I type and we talk. She reads and we talk. We enjoy being together.

Ministry can be intense. Obviously spouses and children can't be around all of the time. Some of my work requires quiet and confidentiality. Some crises are too traumatic or complicated for a child. Competent childcare needs to be available for crises and emergencies. Fortunately, most ministry is predictable and family friendly. My sons, Michael and Aaron, have visited in hospitals with me. They have attended viewings and funerals. They have been with me as I have visited in prisons. They have traveled with me to nursing homes.

They have done door-to-door witnessing. They have visited shut-ins. Many times they have been a greater blessing to the ones we were visiting than I was. Before they were teenagers, sometimes they came with me on youth trips. They have profited by being present while ministry has been taking place. I believe they have learned some great things about life, faith, and ministry. In all the years that I have been pastoring and fathering I have not heard so much as a whisper of objection about me modeling ministry with my children. In fact, many active laypersons in our church have decided to also include their children in ministry. Lonely persons in nursing homes love to be in the presence of our children. Every one is blessed by these multi-generational ministry opportunities.

Pastors and laypersons can do excellent ministry and still have children along. Since this kind of arrangement has worked well for this male pastor for seventeen years, why can't it work for female pastors? It is possible both to be a pastor and to be available as a father. Why is it not also possible to be a pastor and to be available as a mother? Some creative thinking, planning, and scheduling can allow female pastors to spend lots of quality time with their families. One can be both a dedicated pastor and an excellent mother. One can be called both to family and to church ministry. A cooperative church, a flexible spouse, and some creativity is all that it takes.

I think of the example of Dr. Lillie McCutcheon who pastored the Newton Falls Church of God in Ohio from 1945–1988. She led a prosperous and growing congregation yet was also highly committed to her family. Dr. Barry Callen in *She Came Preaching* notes that Pastor McCutcheon invested in both her family and her ministry (1992:159). He writes:

> A busy wife and mother, Lillie was an intensely family oriented person learning to find her way in the sometimes difficult task of balancing the responsibilities of home and church. As had been typical in her family all her life, often the distinction between home and church was intentionally somewhat blurred, and often Lillie's gift of warmth, hospitality, cooking and touching became significant avenues of ministry and church growth (1992:167).

A Biblical Family: Pre-fall and Post-fall Family Types

You stated in your letter that you want a "biblical family." So do I, but what does a biblical family look like? We often assume that a biblical family looks like a 1950s American family. The dad goes out to work. The mom stays home with the kids. The husband makes the major decisions. The woman follows and submits. That picture is more cultural than biblical. Families have always been complex and affected by culture and circumstances. Elizabeth Pistole notes that "Even our grandmothers often found neighbors or relatives to come and stay with the children while they went with the men to work in the field. They were co-pioneers and often were equal partners" (1978:8).

There is no one model biblical family. The Bible was written over a period of many centuries and families were constantly changing with the times. When I study the scriptures I see fundamentally two types of families: the pre-fall family type and post-fall family types. The pre-fall family is God's creative design for the family. It is the family that God prescribes. There is one husband and one wife. There is no hierarchy of any kind in their relationship. God created the husband and wife to complement and complete one another. God gave dominion to both the man and the woman to rule over the earth. They are both commanded to multiply. The husband and wife cling to one another and function as equals. It is the family of paradise.

Post-fall families take many forms. Sin marred human relationships. Blame entered marriage. The curse of sin polluted the earth and brought death and destruction. God declared to the woman, "I will greatly increase your pangs in childbearing; in pain you shall bring forth children, yet your desire shall be for your husband, and he shall rule over you" (Gen 3:16). Women found themselves increasingly under the domination of men. Patriarchy has kept women in submission for centuries. Post-fall families all through the ages have, to varying degrees, been affected by the curse of sin. They are an accommodation to sinful human culture. The Bible describes these fallen families truthfully, but they are not God's original pre-fall prescription.

You want a biblical family. I want a biblical family. When we say that we want biblical families, we need to understand that all post-fall family types are less than what God intended in the Garden of Eden. They are marred by the curse of sin. Let's look at some examples.

When Abraham and Sarah were unable to bear children, Abraham lay with his wife's slave, Hagar, and she bore Abraham and Sarah a child (Gen 16). This family included slaves and sex with a slave. That's a biblical family, but it's not what God intended at creation.

When Isaac was of marrying age, his father Abraham sent his chief servant to his relatives to select a bride for Isaac (Gen 24). That's a biblical family, but

I'm glad that my father didn't have to send his chief slave to my relatives to choose a wife for me.

Jacob married two wives, Rachel and Leah (Gen 29). That's a biblical family but it falls short of God's created design.

David, one of the greatest kings of Israel, had several wives. David committed adultery with Bathsheba and murdered her husband, Uriah the Hittite, to cover it up. Even after this crime David married Bathsheba and kept her as his wife (2 Sam 11). That's a biblical family, but not what God intended in the garden.

Solomon, Israel's most prosperous king, married 700 wives and had 300 concubines (1 Kings 11:11). That's a biblical family but hardly a good example.

Over the centuries, in the Old and New Testaments, the Bible describes families that were marred by the fall. Slave women were taken as wives (Deut 21:10–14). Divorce laws favored men (Deut 24:1–4, Matt 5:31–32; 19:3–12, Luke 16:18). Women were treated as property (Genesis 29:20, Ruth 4:10, Hosea 3:2). Women were under the control and domination of their fathers and their husbands. If a husband died, to protect the dead husband's family line, his brother must marry his widow (Deut 25:5–6). This created polygamy. Women simply were not equals in the patriarchy propagated by the curse of sin. These post-fall families fall short of God's creative intention in the garden.

When I say that I want a biblical family, I am not referring to these post-fall types of family. I am referring to the family that existed before the fall of sin. I am referring to the marriage of two equals, unmarred by the degradation of women brought forth since the fall. I am referring to a marriage where both partners are called to use all their spiritual gifts to love and serve the Lord.

The Male Covering is a Cultural Post-fall Accommodation to a Sinful World

This is a crucial point when we speak of women in ministry because some believe that women must be "under a man's covering" and a woman must always be "under a man's authority." The argument goes "a woman cannot be a senior pastor because she must have the covering of male authority." This is a cultural accommodation to a sinful world. There is no hint of this kind of male authority or hierarchy before the fall. Gilbert Bilezikian notes that "There is nothing in Genesis 1 and 2 that provides even a hint of a disparity of nature or rank between man and woman" (1985:37).

Understanding Male Headship

You mentioned in your letter being under a man's covering and submitting to Mark's headship. What does this really mean? The New Testament contains three passages that refer to male headship (1 Cor 11:1–16, Eph 5:21–33, Col 3:18–19). Philip Barton Payne notes: "The most common error in interpreting 'head' in the Pauline passages is to read back into them the meaning 'leader' " (Mickelsen, 1985:123). Gilbert Bilezikian helpfully describes two different ways of understanding headship. One he calls "hierarchical." The other he calls "chronological" (1985:139). First Corinthians 11:3 says, "But I want you to understand that Christ is the head of every man, and the husband is the head of his wife, and God is the head of Christ." In the hierarchical viewpoint, God is over Christ. Christ is over every man. The husband is over his wife. In the chronological viewpoint, head is viewed as "fountainhead" or "source." We would thus say God is the source of Christ, Christ is the source of every man, and, as Adam was the source of Eve, the husband is the source of his wife. Berkely and Alvera Mickelsen have done extensive research into the meaning of the Greek word *kephale* which is typically translated in English Bibles as "head." They note:

> The most complete Greek-English lexicon (covering Homeric, classical and Koine Greek) in current existence is a two volume work of more than 2,000 pages compiled by Liddell, Scott, Jones and McKenzie, published first in 1843. It is based upon examination of thousands of Greek writings from the period of Homer (about 1000 BC) to about 600 AD, a period of nearly 1600 years, including the Septuagint and New Testament times. This lexicon lists, with examples, the common meanings of *Kephale.* The list includes more than twenty-five possible figurative meanings in addition to the literal meaning of physical head of man or beast. The list does not include, "authority," "superior rank," "leader," "director," or anything similar as a meaning (1985:97–98).

Payne agrees:

> An examination of other Greek lexicons further supports the Mickelsens' thesis. None of the following lexicons lists any examples related to "leader" or "authority": Moulton and

Milligan, Friedrich Preisigke, Pierre Chantraine and E. A. Sophocles gives only one such example from AD 950. S. C. Woodhouse lists twenty Greek equivalents for "chief" or "authority" but *Kephale* is not listed as an equivalent for either of these or for 'leader' (Mickelsen, 1985:118–119).

The notion that "head" should be understood as "superior" or "leader" does not come from the Bible. It is foreign to the Greek. It finds its source in some patristic fathers, John Calvin, and common usage of the English language. The Mickelsens' translate *kephale* as "source of life" in Colossians 2:19 and Ephesians 4:15 (1985:105). *Kephale* is translated as "top" or "crown" in Colossians 2:10 and Ephesians 1:2–23 (1985:106). *Kephale* is "source," "base," or "derivation" in 1 Corinthians 11:3 (1985:106–107). *Kephale* is "exalter," "originator and completer" in Colossians 1:18 (1985:108). *Kephale* is "one who brings to completion" in Ephesians 5:23 (1985:108–109). To argue that male headship means that the man is the woman's leader is to distort God's original intent in marriage.

Janet, Mark is not your boss. He is your mate, your marriage partner. You are both created in God's image. God created you as equals to complement and complete one another. Women do not have to be under the domination, protection, or authority of some male authority. That is accommodation to the fall. Both women and men are free to pastor.

Head Coverings—Keeping Order During Worship

That brings us to the issue of head covering mentioned by the Apostle Paul in 1 Corinthians 11:1–16. The primary concern in this passage is not marriage relationships. Nor is Paul primarily addressing a general need for women to have male covering when they are outside of the home. The issue was keeping order during worship at the Corinthian church. In antiquity, married women commonly wore veils. Prostitutes did not wear veils. They called attention to their beauty by showing their beautiful hair. Not wearing a veil violated the moral sensibility of many common persons. Some wealthier women also chose not to wear veils. When Corinthian women sought to preach or pray without a head covering, they created disharmony in the church. Craig Keener notes, "Head covering prevailed in Jewish Palestine (where it extended even to a face veil) and elsewhere, but upper class women eager to show off their fashionable hairstyles did not practice it. Thus Paul must address a clash of culture between upper-class fashion and lower-class concern that sexual propriety is being violated" (1993:475). The issue was a concern for unity and order in worship within a particular cultural context. Women today are free to exercise all of their spiritual gifts in the church without requiring a male head covering.

Ethical Issues for Female Pastors

In your letter, you suggested that it is not ethically appropriate for men and women to work together. I admit that some relationships do lead to improprieties. This even happens with women who stay at home. Many stay-at-home moms have had affairs. Temptations need not prohibit persons from exercising their spiritual gifts in ministry. Women do not need to be locked up in the home. Men and women must relate with propriety everywhere they go. We shop at the same stores. We attend the same doctors' offices. We travel on the same sidewalks. We camp in the same campgrounds. We fly on the same airplanes. We ride on the same buses. We attend the same parent meetings for PTA, soccer, and little league. We worship in the same congregations. Why should we focus upon the potential pitfalls of women pastors working with men or with other male pastors?

Is it equally improper for male pastors to work with female secretaries? Is it equally improper for male doctors to work with female nurses? Is it equally improper for male school principals to work with female teachers? Men and women live and work with one another at all levels of society. These working relationships need not lead to adultery when appropriate boundaries are maintained. Men and women can worship together, shop in the same stores, and work together when they maintain ethical integrity.

Janet, you and I are friends. Our friendship is entirely appropriate. I respect that you are married to Mark and you respect that I am married to Susan. We have a healthy relationship as a sister and brother in the Lord. You respect and value my spiritual gifts and I respect and value yours. As I see it, we both are free to exercise our spiritual gifts for the benefit of the church. You do not have to avoid your Christian brothers or use your spiritual gifts only in your home to have ethically appropriate relationships. You can be both a godly mother and serve and lead in the church. There is no more danger of ethical impropriety for women pastors working with men than there is for male pastors working with women. We all must function with integrity.

Janet, I want to repeat that I respect your decision to be a stay-at-home mom. I only ask that you understand that other women who love their husbands and children are called to be leaders in God's church. These women are both excellent pastors and homemakers. They deserve our support and respect. I respect every person, male or female, who says "yes" to being a godly parent. I also respect every person, male or female, who says "yes" to God's call to be a pastor. I believe this is God's will.

I'd be glad to talk with you more about this. Thank you so much for sharing your views with me. May God bless you and your family.

In Christian Love,

Pastor Randy

Discussion Questions for Chapter 6

1. What is the biblical evidence that, in addition to domestic roles, God also calls women to other important responsibilities?

2. The author discusses several child-care options for female pastors. Which of these seem most feasible? What other options might work well for women pastors?

3. The author makes distinctions between the pre-fall family type and post-fall family types. What are the characteristics of the pre-fall family?

4. In what ways do various post-fall family types fall short of God's pre-fall design?

5. What is the author's understanding of male headship?

6. Since *kephale*, the Greek term commonly translated as head, does not imply authority, how does that affect many common views of male and female relationships?

7. What is the evidence that head coverings for women were an accommodation for specific women in a particular time and culture?

8. How do you respond to the argument that it is unethical for women pastors to work with men?

9. How could families in the local church benefit by having a female pastor?

A Woman Couldn't Do It

Chapter 7

Dear Randy,

    As you know, I'm on the pulpit committee at our church. I have hesitated to contact you because I know you don't agree with what I'm about to say. I have been afraid that you would judge me for what I honestly believe. I had to write anyway because I take my responsibility on the pulpit committee seriously. We have received a few resumes from women. These women have good educations and great references.

    I just don't think a woman can cut it in the ministry. I question that a woman could really be competent. I see so many disadvantages. They have husbands and children to care for. They could get pregnant. They won't be accepted by some of our men. Our men's group wouldn't respect a woman pastor. Frankly, I don't think our women's group would respect a woman pastor either. I believe some people might leave the church if we had a woman pastor. Women are too emotional to handle the daily pressures. Even if I were persuaded that God allows women to be pastors, I'm just not convinced that a woman could really do the job. Thanks for listening. I'm open to what you have to say. I've shared my honest feelings.

In His Service,

James

Dear James:

Thanks so much for sharing your honest feelings with me. Our society has a lot of ambivalence about what women can or cannot do. Years of stereotyping and prejudice die hard.

Childhood Experiences Affect Our Views on the Capabilities of Women

I remember when I was growing up the kinds of remarks that boys made to one another. "We don't want him on our team. He throws like a girl!" "He's a wimp. He got beat up by a girl." "Don't hit him; he cries like a girl." The worst thing one boy could call another was "girl." The ultimate insult was to be defeated by a girl in anything. Girls, too, grow up in this competitive environment where boys struggle to dominate on the playground. Many girls are also poisoned by playground culture. I know many women who, despite outstanding capabilities, do not believe that they can be as capable as a man. They have never grown beyond the immature notions of the playground pecking order.

Propagating Gender Stereotypes

Sometimes our society seeks to propagate gender-based stereotypes. I am not saying that men and women are the same. Clearly there are biological differences, but our prevailing culture and parenting practices also have a great effect upon perpetuating gender stereotypes. Some of those stereotypes are changing. Few persons today would still claim that women are incapable of driving a car, voting, practicing law, serving in Congress, or practicing medicine. Not all women want to be rescued "damsels in distress." Some want to be fire fighters and rescue workers. Our Lord Jesus Christ was a strong leader. He also wept at the grave of his friend Lazarus. Being a strong leader is not necessarily "for men only." Nor is weeping necessarily "for women only."

Men and women share many common experiences, feelings, and traits. Sometimes men are better nurturers than women. Sometimes women are better leaders than men. Some women are moody. Some men are equally moody. I know insensitive men. I also know insensitive women. The spiritual fruit described in Galatians 5:22–23 is neither male nor female. Both men and women, when filled with the Holy Spirit, become loving, joyful, peaceful, patient, gentle, good, faithful, meek, and self-controlled. Sometimes the bold prophetic preacher is male; however, many times I have heard the prophetic voice of Jeannette Flynn, the director of Congregational Ministries of the Church of God. Her preaching has challenged me. Sometimes the ministry of my male friends meets my needs. Other times God uses a woman. I remember attending a visioning conference for the Church of God in Colorado Springs. I carried some heavy burdens. My wife was battling cancer. I shared my concerns with several of my male pastoral colleagues who listened politely but failed to respond to my need. I shared with Esther Cottrell, a highly capable pastor that I have known since seminary days. Esther alone saw my hurt, put her arm around me, and prayed for me. All of my male friends were competent pastors, but only Esther responded at the level of my need. Was it because Esther was a woman that she met my need? Perhaps Esther's socialization as a woman aided her in being more sensitive than my male friends. More importantly, Esther met my need because she is full of the Holy Spirit and she loved with Christ's love. Neither male nor female has a corner on the Holy Spirit or the love of Christ. Males are not automatically competent because they are male. Females are not automatically incompetent because they are female.

God Calls, Equips, and Uses Women Pastors and Leaders

Regardless of our perceptions about the alleged inabilities of women, the truth is that throughout the history of the Church of God, women have performed outstanding ministry. It hurts the church when we hold women back from ministry. C. W. Naylor, in the April 25, 1918 issue of *The Gospel Trumpet,* noted: "There are today multitudes of souls who have been brought to Christ through the ministry of faithful, Spirit-anointed women. To condemn their work in such a capacity is to condemn the God whose blessing is upon their labors and who saves souls who hear them. Beware lest you fight against God." James, I believe my best response to your letter is to share some names and stories that demonstrate, despite your misgivings, that women *can* do it. Women have served and are serving all over the church as highly capable pastors and leaders.

In a May 1, 1977 *Vital Christianity* article titled "The Status of Women in the Church," Anna E. Koglin wrote: "The pioneers of the Church of God, such as D. S. Warner, considered women equal to men. Women were a part of the evangelizing teams. They served as exhorters and counselors. Somewhat later they also served as evangelists and pastors. They have been highly successful too." All through the history of the Church of God women have demonstrated their considerable capabilities.

Joseph Allison provides this list: Tillie Craft, Edith A. Trask, Burd Barwick and Marie Schaffer, Amanda Brown, Mrs. S. J. Tosh, Bertha Rowe, Rosa Kilpatrick, Jane Williams, Mrs. L. Reed, Mrs. T. A. Duncan, Ada B. Parkins, Naomi Shelton, Dassie M. Pye, Anna Koglin, Alice Sprague, Lottie Charles, Viola Brown, Gertrude Carter, Mae McAlpine, Effie Lavell, Sydney and Delcie Pauley, Emma and Willa Myers, Lena Shoffner Matthesen, L. W. and Claudine Guilford, Rachel Bailey Rawlinson, Pearl Kemp, Mamie Bosconer and Lura Farmer as having held evangelistic meetings in the early days of the Church of God (1978:22). Allison adds that following World War I women moved away from evangelistic work toward becoming pastors of congregations. "Esther Boyer, Bertha Gaulke, May Frazee, Zuda Chambers Rothman, Sarah Massey McCain, Hazel G. Neal, Emma Coulbourne, Emma Burgess, Nora S. Hunter and many others could be mentioned as pastors of vital churches in the 1920s and 1930s" (1978:23). As the decades have passed, the Church of God has been blessed with numerous capable women who have pastored and led the church.

Allison laments:

> Women virtually disappeared from the pastoral scene in the 1950s and 1960s, with a few important exceptions such as Pastor Lillie S. McCutcheon of Newton Falls, Ohio, and Pastor Pauline Maxwell of Hamilton, Ohio. Most women pastors in recent years have been found in black congregations or very small white congregations—situations in which they received part-time salaries or none at all, relying upon their husband's income for the necessities of life (1978:23).

Lillie McCutcheon

The first highly capable woman pastor that I ever met was Dr. Lillie McCutcheon. I quickly learned that she possessed great grace and charm. She was a highly intelligent, capable leader and communicator. Barry Callen wrote an excellent biography on her life titled *She Came Preaching*. Reverend McCutcheon served from 1945 to 1988 as senior pastor at the Newton Falls, Ohio congregation of the Church of God. This congregation prospered under her ministry. The *1988 Yearbook of the Church of God* records that average

Sunday morning worship attendance was 574 persons. During her pastorate she conducted two thousand funerals. For nine years she did a weekly television ministry. She was in high demand as a convention and camp meeting speaker. Callen notes that she published two books, two book portions, twenty-seven articles, and many other publications (1992:315–316). The Newton Falls congregation mentored dozens of persons into pastoral ministry, associate pastoral ministry, national leadership positions, and Christian higher education (1992:324). Jeannette Flynn, the Director of Congregational Ministries for Church of God Ministries said, "Sister Lillie forever will be molding my life. Memories of her teaching and her living constantly instruct and sometimes caution me" (1992:307). Callen believes Sister Lillie was successful because "she had a rich heritage, strong convictions, a clear calling, a genuine heart for people and strong hands that didn't retreat from anything that needed to be done" (1992:163). Dr. Lillie McCutcheon is remembered and revered all over the church. She certainly demonstrates that a woman can be an effective pastor and leader.

The Church of God is also blessed with many outstanding pastors and leaders who are currently serving the church. All are highly capable women. Consider the following:

Dana D. Brown[3]

Dana Brown has demonstrated considerable ability and a willingness to serve her Lord. Her past experience encompasses being personnel director for a manufacturing firm, law enforcement chaplaincy, and chaplaincy designing in Ohio. She has also served in church associate positions and as treasurer of the Indiana North Association of the Church of God. Additionally, she has served on the Indiana Board of Church Growth and Health and as an Anderson University trustee.

Brown responded to God's call to ministry October 25, 1990. She has a degree in business management from Oklahoma State University and graduated from Anderson University School of Theology in 1994. Brown was ordained to ministry in 1995.

Dana Brown deeply values the mentoring of others who have aided her in fulfilling her call. She wrote:

> One of my mentors is the past dean of the Anderson University School of Theology, Dr. James Earl Massey. During

the course of our conversation in his office, he pointed to a picture on the wall and asked me to describe it to him. It was a watercolor (so the colors were subtle). You could tell that the viewer was inside some building (probably a barn) and you could see the hillside in the distance with a small church on the hill. In describing this scene to Dr. Massey, he asked, "Yes, but what are you looking through?" I realized then that the window pane the viewer was looking through was broken. He responded, "Always remember, Ms. Brown, that through the brokenness, you can still see hope." That was my "Paul-and-Timothy" moment and I realized that I had just been given my charge. Thus I had my mission.

For nearly four years Brown has served as senior pastor of First Church of God in LaPorte, Indiana. The *2002 Yearbook of the Church of God* indicates that this congregation averages 258 persons in Sunday morning worship. Brown describes the congregation as "a wonderful congregation that has come far in the almost four years that I've served here." She demonstrates a sensible and realistic approach to the challenges of life and ministry. She notes, "Through each and every experience there has been trial, triumph, frustration, success, betrayal and support." Due to her gender, there were some bumpy times at the beginning of her pastorate in LaPorte, but Brown notes that now "the congregation has fully embraced me as a leader and as a person." She has a healthy and refreshing understanding of the challenges of being a woman pastor. She wrote to me:

> My philosophy of my gender is that I will not be a political issue. In other words, while I have no problem discussing my calling to anyone who asks, I will not debate whether a woman can or cannot be called into ministry. To me, that is what the Bible calls "vain arguments." My philosophy has been to simply love people (despite what they think about my calling) and be faithful to what God has called me to, and then to allow the Holy Spirit to change hearts.

This approach is clearly working for her. Brown also wrote to me:

> Probably the best compliment I have ever received was from a man whose family had returned to the church. He came into

my office and said, "Pastor, I have to confess that when we returned to the church and saw that you were the senior pastor, I had a problem with you being a woman in such a position. So I prayed about it. And the Lord helped me to see past your gender, and see your heart. You are my pastor and you have my support." I was honored with such an accolade.

At the beginning of her ministry, one of Brown's mentors, Dr. Lillie McCutcheon, told her, "Remember, Dana, God knew your gender when he called you to ministry. So don't apologize for it. God has a plan for it. Don't try to be anything or anyone else than yourself. Simply be a lady in the pulpit, be Dana in the pulpit. That will be enough."

Mary Ann Hawkins[4]

Mary Ann Hawkins married her husband, James, in 1973. They have two grown children, Alysia and Timothy. Mary Ann serves as associate pastor in administration and music at South Bay Church of God in Torrance, California. James serves as senior pastor at the same congregation. South Bay Church of God averages over 200 persons in Sunday morning worship attendance. Mary Ann also serves as the chair of the Credentials Committee for the Church of God in Southern California and Southern Nevada. She is the first female to serve on this committee in Southern California. Under her leadership, the committee is currently redesigning its credentials process to include mentoring.

Hawkins began formal ministry in 1985. This followed ten years of what she describes as being a "*very* active pastor's wife." She notes, "God called me specifically to a ministry *of my own, that would 'walk' with my husband's ministry* in 1984." Since that time she served on church staff with James at East Tulsa Church of God in Tulsa, Oklahoma. She served as faculty and academic dean at Kima International School of Theology (KIST) in Kenya, and as faculty at Hope International University (HIU) in Fullerton, California. Hope International University is a Christian school affiliated with the independent Christian Churches. During her time at HIU the number of students declaring an Intercultural Studies major quadrupled and Hawkins negotiated covenant relationships with two mission organizations to provide internships for these students. She is firm in her call. Her call to ministry was confirmed during a conference led by Carolyn Waddy Reid at Anderson Convention, June 1985.[5]

Mary Ann Hawkins is a highly gifted person. Not only has she ministered in demanding academic positions, but she is also currently pursuing a Ph.D. in Intercultural Studies (Leadership) at the School of World Mission, Fuller Theological Seminary. She plans to graduate in June 2003.

When I began my studies of women in ministry several persons told me, "You have got to get in contact with Mary Ann Hawkins." Hawkins has done extensive and helpful research on women ministers in the Church of God. She has been helpful to me.

For those who question whether women can be competent leaders, Hawkins clearly demonstrates consistent skill. During 1994, she served as acting principal (college president) for missionary Don Armstrong at the Babati Bible School in Tanzania. Kenya, like most African nations, is highly patriarchal. It is a testimony to her competency that it was a male Kenyan who suggested that in 1997 she take on the responsibilities of the academic dean at Kima International School of Theology. Hawkins had earned the right to speak and lead by demonstrating excellence as a faculty member at Kima Theological College. When Steve Rennick and his family left Kenya for furlough, Mary Ann continued as dean at KIST. During that time, Kima International School of Theology completed two building projects, hired two new faculty members (one male, one female), expanded their dairy herd, and completed the primary requirements toward offering an accredited degree. During this time, Hawkins' preaching and teaching schedule was as active as her husband's who also was on faculty at Kima International School of Theology. Mary Ann Hawkins serves her Lord with competence and grace. She clearly demonstrates that "women can do it."

Mandy Stanley[6]

I first met Mandy Stanley while she was a student in seminary. Her parents, John and Susie Stanley, attend the church that I pastor. Later, Mandy Stanley served one summer as an informal intern with us at Chapel Hill Church of God. I discovered that she is highly intelligent, highly motivated, and a gifted preacher. She is a keen observer and a quick learner. She won our hearts as a warm, responsive, and capable person.

Stanley grew up as the daughter of two ordained ministers. Her father pastored until she was five, then both of her parents attended graduate school to work on their doctorates. Today, John and Susie Stanley serve the church primarily as professors. Mandy Stanley wrote, "While some shudder at the thought of living in a house with two ministers, for me it has been an enriching experience. My parents provided me the environment to develop my own faith and beliefs." She came to faith early, making a commitment to God during a summer camp at age seven. While she attended seminary she become reacquainted with her Sunday school teacher from preschool. Her teacher told her of the questions she asked as a four year old in her early pursuit of knowledge about God.

Stanley writes of her call to ministry.

> I heard the call of God on my life to be a medical missionary during my junior high years. I prepared for this call by filling my life with extra science courses and extracurricular activities related to medicine. I enrolled in college and spent two years pursuing a premed degree. I began to hear God redirecting me my sophomore year of college. I knew that a change was needed. I changed my major to Spanish language and planned for a life as a bilingual minister.

Stanley has a global vision of the church. She has no hang-ups about race or culture, gender or socio-economic class. She believes and practices that the Church of God embraces persons from every corner of the globe. She entered seminary with the desire to enhance her studies with interaction from the Hispanic community in the USA. She chose Wesley Theological Seminary due to its diversity and because it allowed her to intern with Spanish- speaking congregations.

During the last year of her Master of Divinity degree Stanley served as interim pastor in Beaver, Pennsylvania. After graduation she accepted a call to Tokyo Union Church where she has served as associate pastor since August 2000. Parishioners come from around the world and from just about every denomination to worship together in this large congregation. She notes, "My time with TUC has increased my belief that what the world needs are ecumenical efforts to spread the Gospel and demonstrate the unity that we have in Christ."

Stanley reflects with gratitude that her experience at TUC has been unique. She has had little experience of being rejected for being a woman. "People assume that if one is brought from the US to work in Tokyo, they have the skills required for the job." Mandy wrote to me, "One family had previously been against women in ministry. After worshiping at TUC they decided that women could be called and equipped by God in the same way that men are equipped." She noted that this kind of attitude "fuels me for the days when I do hear negative comments or questions wondering if TUC could have two women on pastoral staff."

Stanley loves to teach. One of the highlights of her ministry in Tokyo has been teaching an adult Bible study. She writes: "About ten of us read 85 percent of the Bible in nine months. The group was composed of people from five countries bringing their traditions and experiences to the study. It was a wonderful time of fellowship and spiritual growth. We truly can be one in Christ."

I had the pleasure of attending Mandy Stanley's ordination. As we prayed over her and affirmed her call, I had a sense of joy that our Lord has uniquely prepared Mandy to serve cross culturally in the church. The church needs many more leaders with Mandy's vision. Mandy Stanley is a gifted leader in the kingdom of God.

Barbara Olivia Brooks Berry[7]

Since 1999, Barbara Berry has served as associate pastor of pastoral care at North Anderson Church of God in Anderson, Indiana. The North Anderson congregation is one of the largest and most progressive congregations in the Church of God. The *2002 Yearbook of the Church of God* records that, on average, over 2000 persons attend Sunday morning worship. Berry is an African-American pastor serving in an essentially all white environment. She indicates, "The members are very respectful, warm, loving, and accepting."

Reverend Berry is well prepared for ministry. She was ordained to ministry in 1994. Her education includes an Associate of Science Degree in Business (1976), a Bachelor of Arts Degree in Management (Organizational Theory and Human Resources) (1992), and a Master of Divinity from Anderson University School of Theology (1999). Her Master of Divinity specialized in pastoral care.

Barbara is the fifth child of seven children born to the Berrys in San Francisco, California and raised in Marin City just north of the Golden Gate Bridge. Her parents divorced before she entered school. Her mother raised her as a Catholic but her father also raised her in the Marin City Church of God.

1970 was a big year for Barbara Berry. She moved to Oklahoma as a new bride and was converted to Christ in a strict Baptist church in Oklahoma. She learned that she did not need a human priest to receive God's forgiveness. She could "go to Jesus directly." In June, 1970 Berry returned to California and again attended the Marin City Church of God. While her husband served in Viet Nam, she "grew in grace and the knowledge of the Lord" and "received the infilling of the Holy Spirit." Berry began working with youth and Sunday school. Performing various ministries over the years, she identified and developed her "spiritual gifts of exhortation, teaching, administration/organization, and prophecy."

Barbara Berry wrote to me,

> For years I had visions/dreams of myself standing preaching the Word of God, winning souls to Christ, but I did not acknowledge my call to anyone. However, many in the congregation affirmed I was called to ministry. I was in denial. One Sunday afternoon a guest evangelist at prayer time called me forward and asked me openly, "Did I know God had called me to preach?" I replied, "Yes." This was the first time I publicly acknowledged my call.

Berry deeply appreciates her father who many times encouraged her to pursue her call. She also values the examples and encouragement of other women pastors in the San Francisco Bay Area: Sarah Pointer, Willa Mae Tires, Betty Rogers, Dr. Cynthia James, and Wilma Brooks (her step-mother).

Like most other women ministers, Berry has from time to time experienced opposition to her ministry. Once when she was attending a Bay Area ministerial meeting a prominent Church of God leader told her that he did not believe in women pastors. Berry was "shocked and upset." She told me of the experience.

> He asked me, "why would a woman want to be a pastor?" I explained, "I did not want to be a pastor, but God has a call on my life and I must be obedient. I did not wake-up one morning and say, 'Oh I think I will be a preacher/pastor.' " This seminary educated COG pastor admitted that biblically he could not prove women should not be in ministry.

It is amazing that Berry can add, "Today this pastor is one of my greatest encouragers and confidants."

While in seminary in 1999, her Master of Divinity program required three units of Clinical Pastoral Education (CPE) as a chaplain. Sometimes Berry ministered to persons who did not believe in women clergy. In these situations, she did not address their comments. She focused on them and their illness. Berry wrote to me, "I have learned early in ministry not to argue, debate, or even expend energy in discussing women in ministry. I just ministered if people allowed me to, and watched the Holy Spirit work. If there is hostility, I just shake the dust from my feet and hands and move on. Only God can touch and change people's opinions and hearts."

Over the years, in addition to her service at Marin City Church of God, she has served as an interim pastor and senior pastor of the First Church of God in Napa, California. Berry has demonstrated remarkable strength and courage in her ministry. In 1988, the year that she was first licensed as a Church of God minister, after nineteen years of marriage she was widowed. Yet she served the church and raised her two sons as a single parent. Clearly, Barbara O. Berry demonstrates that, even in difficult circumstances, a woman can be an effective pastor.

Barbara Deale Miller[8]

Barbara Deale Miller served twenty-two years as a missionary of the Church of God in Bolivia, South America. The daughter of United Methodist missionaries, she was raised in Zaire and Zimbabwe. As a teenager, Miller experienced a "definite call to ministry." God confirmed her call as a call to cross-cultural ministry at an Urbana Missions Conference when she was eighteen. Miller graduated with a Bachelor of Arts degree from Asbury College and a Master of Divinity degree from Asbury Theological Seminary. She was president of the seminary senior class in 1978.

Like most women, Miller has faced some discrimination in her ministry. While a seminary student, she took clinical pastoral education. She writes: "Once, while working at a hospital in Columbus, Ohio, I walked into a patient's room and introduced myself as the chaplain. He literally laughed in my face and exclaimed, 'You are not the chaplain!' I guess I did not quite fit his stereotype."

Barbara married Dave Miller and six months later Barbara and Dave Miller were Church of God missionaries in Bolivia. Miller tells of her experience as a female missionary.

> Living and working in Bolivia was a lesson in balancing biblical and cultural principles. The Church of God in Bolivia

> does not believe in women pastors, does not permit women to preach (except some missionary types) and has definite ideas about a woman's place in the church. I did not wish to usurp my husband's credibility and/or position with the church, so I tried to work within biblical guidelines while not upsetting the cultural norms unnecessarily—not an easy task. I learned a lot about humility. I concentrated on the doors open to me—teaching, counseling, mentoring, discipling mostly women and some youth. Little by little, year by year, the barriers were broken down by being an example of what God can do in a person's life, no matter what sex they happen to be. On several occasions I was asked to preach for the whole church and participate in pastoral training.

Working within limiting cultural restraints, Miller was successful in helping some men and women to accept a broader understanding of women's roles in the church. She especially helped Indian women to understand that God gives spiritual gifts to both men and women. Reflecting upon her ministry as a leader in the church in Bolivia, Miller writes:

> At one of the farewells hosted by the church, several women gave their testimonies and thanked me, with tears in their eyes for setting them free to be active in the church. That was an affirmation to me that my labors were not in vain and that women in the Church of God in Bolivia will be helping in many ways to build up the church. My life's verse is Galatians 5:1: "It is for freedom that Christ has set us free. Stand firm, then, and do not let yourself be burdened again by a yoke of slavery." Amen.

Miller is a dedicated leader who served for twenty-two years in a culture that was not her own. She is a wise and courageous pioneer catalyzing theological and cultural change. Barbara Deale Miller is a faithful and capable leader in the Church of God.

Cheryl Sanders[9]

Sanders is an intelligent and articulate professor, preacher, author, lecturer, and pastor. God called her to ministry while she was a student in college. She began her theological studies three years after graduation. In her early years she was active in her local church while focusing upon campus and youth ministries. She wrote to me:

> I have continually been blessed by a number of persons who have encouraged me in my ministry over the years. It was good for me to grow up in a church that did not debate or dispute the leadership roles of women, and I have been able to function as a pioneer in ministry settings where a woman's preaching and leadership had not been received before. One of the greatest blessings in my life has been the love and support of family, beginning with my parents and my brother, later my husband, and also our two children. My children are brutal critics of sermons and worship, so they keep me on my toes.

She earned her Doctor of Theology in Applied Theology from Harvard Divinity School. Sanders was ordained to Church of God ministry in 1981. She served two years as interim pastor at First Church of God in Boston, Massachusetts. Since 1984, she has been professor of Christian ethics at Howard University School of Divinity. She was awarded the honorary Doctor of Divinity degree in 2002 by Asbury College.

For more than seven years, Sanders served on pastoral staff at Third Street Church of God in Washington, DC, a church that averages two hundred persons in Sunday morning worship attendance and is respected across the country. When former senior pastor, Dr. Samuel G. Hines, died, Sanders was assigned the responsibilities of senior pastor. She has led this congregation since May of 1997. Many experts affirm that seldom can a new pastor successfully follow the tenure of a long-term beloved pastor. Sanders has succeeded in following one of the most beloved and respected pastors and leaders in the Church of God. This is a great testament to her considerable capabilities and the manner in which she has endeared herself to the Third Street Church.

In addition to her pastoral and teaching responsibilities Sanders also serves as First Vice-Chairperson of the Mayor's Interfaith Council in Washington, DC. She is a lecturer for the Summer Leadership Institute at Harvard Divinity School, and involved in the Executive Session on Faith-Based and Community Approaches to Urban Revitalization, Kennedy School of Government, Harvard University. She is a member of the Advisory Board, Pew Forum on Religion and Public Life, and of the Governance Committee, National Association of the Church of God. She also serves on the National

Steering Committee, SHAPE (Sustaining Health and Pastoral Excellence) Initiative of the Church of God and participates in the Research Think Tank, Howard University. Additionally, she is a member of the Ministers Council, Chesapeake-Delaware-Potomac District of the Church of God.

Sanders has regular opportunities to share her perspectives at the highest levels of American government. She recently met with Senator Majority Leader Bill Frist to discuss public policy and health care. She has been invited to the White House on numerous occasions from 1993 to the present. She was a participant in the Ethics Working Group in the Health Care Reform effort led by then—First Lady Hilary Clinton, and as recently as last May stood with several clergy persons of various faiths to watch President Bush sign the Clergy Housing Allowance Clarification Act. Weeks before his inauguration, President-Elect Bush invited Sanders to a briefing in Austin, Texas and she had the opportunity to engage him in a conversation about empathy and advocacy for the poor. She was invited to be Guest Chaplain in the House of Representatives and when she offered the opening prayer she was introduced on the floor of the House and her biography was entered into the Congressional Record. God continues to open doors of opportunity for her to advocate for the poor and for the cause of Christ in the corridors of power. When considering her gender in ministry she wrote:

> I have always known women ministers and pastors in the Church of God. I never wondered whether women should preach or not. It is evident to me that, all things being equal, a man with my qualifications and gifts would have many more opportunities and would earn more compensation than I do. However, it is my conviction that the God who called me has made a way for me to fulfill that calling beyond my dreams and imagination. So I do what I can to mentor and encourage other women who are finding their way in ministry, and want to advocate for congregations to be more open to women when seeking pastors and staffing ministries.

Sanders is in high demand as a visiting professor and preacher. She is a well-respected scholar. Sanders is also the author of numerous articles and several books. She is a contributing editor of *Leadership Journal* published for pastors by *Christianity Today*. Among her books are: *Empowerment Ethics for a Liberated People, Living the Intersection: Womanism and Afro-Centrism in Theology, Saints in Exile: the Holiness-Pentecostal Experience in African*

American Religion and Culture, and Ministry at the Margins; The Prophetic Mission of Women, Youth, and Poor. Dr. Cheryl Sanders clearly demonstrates that women can be highly effective pastors and leaders.

Rita J. Johnson[10]

Rita J. Johnson has been a Christian since she was nine years old. God called her into ministry when she was sixteen. She spent many years as an evangelist preaching across the United States, Canada, Bermuda, and Africa, while raising a family and running the family insurance business. She has served on numerous local, state, and national boards within the Church of God. Johnson is a graduate of William Tyndale Bible College with an Associate of Arts in Religious Studies, Spring Arbor College with a Bachelor of Arts in Human Resources, and Southern California School of Ministry with a Masters in Ministry. She also received an honorary Doctor of Divinity from Southern California School of Ministry.

Johnson currently serves as senior pastor of the Sumpter Community Church of God in Belleville, Michigan. Altogether, she has pastored there for twenty-two years—three years as interim pastor and nineteen years as senior pastor. As an interim pastor, Johnson struggled with whether God permits women to be pastors. She writes, "In several personal encounters God assured me he was not discriminatory in giving gifts and that the gift of pastoring was not exclusive to men." With the issue settled in her own soul, Johnson accepted the call to pastor this church of approximately twenty-eight members in the rural Belleville area in 1983. Over the course of the next ten years the congregation grew to over one hundred twenty-five members. Since their building comfortably held only about ninety members, Johnson led the church in purchasing twenty acres and in 1995 built a 350 seat sanctuary. Since then the fellowship has grown to over 600 persons, prompting the congregation to build again. Johnson has successfully led this congregation from a tiny nucleus of persons to a thriving congregation built upon the cell church model. Sumpter Community Church of God is a very diverse congregation where old and young, rich and poor, professional and blue collar, all joins together in worship and outreach.

Johnson reflects upon her role as a female pastor:

> There is a very strong foundation of men who submit to leadership and inspire, comfort and encourage me to do and be all that God has made me. In our local fellowship I have not

encountered the stereotypes that are sometimes attached to women, such as "women are too emotional," "men will not respect women leaders, etc." I receive full respect and support from the men in our congregation who are doctors, dentists, businessmen, professional athletes, principals, counselors, teachers, and others that many would think could not submit to female leadership.

Johnson is a capable pastor in the Church of God. God is using her mightily. She is an irrefutable demonstration that women can be highly effective pastors. Rita Johnson is a great gift to the church.

James, we could explore the ministry contributions of literally hundreds of women who are making an impact upon the church. Richard Goode wrote, "We are blessed in our movement with some wonderful pastors who just happen to be female. Only the God of eternity is fully aware of all the tremendous ministry being done by women" (1989:21). The more that I have studied women in ministry, the more I am deeply impressed by the capabilities of our Christian sisters.

In a 1939 issue of *The Gospel Trumpet*, C. E. Brown, who edited the *Gospel Trumpet* from 1930–1951, wrote:

> Probably one of the greatest sources of the weakness of the modern church is that it has refused women the opportunity for distinguished service within its ranks. By thus closing the door in the face of millions of its most talented and consecrated workers it has diverted their strength into hundreds of other social agencies and thus robbed itself of an incalculable influence in the modern world.

I am in awe at the thought of what the church will become when we fully embrace the calling of capable women in the church. Our best years will be ahead.

James, as you can see, women can be highly effective pastors and leaders. May God aid your congregation as you seek an effective pastor. You may discover that the most-qualified person is a woman.

In Christian love,

Randy

Discussion Questions for Chapter 7

1. To what extent do you believe our childhood experiences affect our opinions about the capabilities of women?

2. To what extent does gender stereotyping hinder the ministry of women?

3. To what extent does gender stereotyping hinder the ministry of men?

4. How do the illustrations of capable female pastors and leaders in this chapter refute the argument that women cannot be capable pastors or leaders?

5. Who are some capable female pastors or leaders that you respect?

A Modern Feminist Thing

Chapter 8

Dear Reverend Huber:

I accepted Christ as a young boy when my parents became friends with an English missionary. I was educated in an excellent missionary-operated school that prepared me to further my education in the United States. Growing up in Asia, nearly everyone understood the proper roles of men and women. I was taught that God intends for men to lead and for women to follow. I immigrated to the United States in 1957. When I first came to America, Americans were also clear about male and female roles. Since the early 1960s I have witnessed American society unravel. I believe one of the greatest factors in that unraveling is feminism. Feminists have brought increased divorce rates, more abortions, sexual promiscuity, lesbianism, goddess worship, witchcraft, and gender confusion into American homes. Feminism has undermined much that has made America great.

Now you are putting forward a feminist agenda by wanting women to be pastors. Your effort to encourage female leadership in the church is a modern feminist thing. You are making a grave mistake. We need to follow the Bible, not feminism. The Bible should set the agenda, not the feminists. Worldly philosophies like feminism are destroying the church, the home, and our nation. I hope that you will return to the Bible as your source of authority and renounce this feminist nonsense. It's unbiblical and it's dangerous.

I am told that you are a reasonable man. I wish you God's blessings as you study further.

Sincerely,

Dr. Li Chang

Dear Dr. Chang:

Thank you for expressing your views to me. I hope that I am a reasonable man. I strive to be both biblically based and intellectually honest. We agree that the Bible should set our agenda but we arrive at different conclusions about women in ministry. I believe that women should not be hindered from pursuing their calls to ministry. I base this view not in feminism, but in the Bible.

Feminism Defined

For clarity in our discussion I will seek to define feminism. Feminism is a broad movement with a long history. Catherine Clark Kroeger, in an article titled "Toward an Egalitarian Hermeneutic of Faith," writes, "In its initial dictionary meaning, it means a person who believes in the equality of men and women" Using that simple definition, I am a feminist. I prefer to call myself a biblical feminist because my belief in the equality of men and women comes from the Bible and everything that I affirm about women in ministry is biblical.

Your letter contained a great deal of stereotyping. Not all feminists are non-Christians. Many feminists love the Lord Jesus Christ and are deeply committed to scripture. Neither are all feminists Christians. Some feminists hold views with which you and I would likely disagree. I recently read a book written by two young feminists that we would agree contains some non-biblical elements. In *Manifesta: Young Women, Feminism and the Future*, Jennifer Baumgardner and Amy Richards attempt to re-energize feminism. They call themselves "Third Wave" Feminists. They write: "What weaves a feminist movement together is consciousness of inequities and a commitment to changing them" (2000:48). Their understanding of feminism is quite broad. They add, "By feminists, we mean each and every politically and socially conscious woman or man who works for equality within or outside the movement, writes about feminism, or calls her or himself a feminist in the name of furthering equality. In reality there is no formal alliance of women we call 'the feminists'" (2000:54).

Baumgardner and Richards make sense when they say: "In the most basic sense, feminism is exactly what the dictionary says it is: the movement for social, political, and economic equality of men and women. Public opinion polls confirm that when women are given this definition, 71 percent say they agree with feminism, along with 61 percent of men" (2000:56). Baumgardner and Richards believe in a expansive feminist tent. Some persons in that tent maintain a biblical worldview and others do not. I do not base my case for women in ministry upon Baumgardner, Richards, or any feminist. I base my case upon the Bible.

Biblical Equality, Not Radical Feminism

Some in the church stereotype feminists as being anti-God, anti-family, anti-man and anti-life. Some outspoken feminists may fit that description but stereotyping does a disservice to biblical feminists who base their views upon the Holy Bible. Some Christians use their stereotype-driven moral indignation as a rationale to oppose women in ministry. They need to leave their stereotypes against feminism behind and return to the Bible. In the Church of God we sing a hymn that says, "The Bible is our rule of faith and Christ alone is Lord, / All we are equal in his sight when we obey His Word."[11] God created both women and men in the divine image and gave them dominion over the earth. There was no hierarchy of any kind between men and women at creation. Both men and women should be allowed to exercise all of their spiritual gifts. This isn't radical feminism; this is biblical teaching.

Focusing upon non-biblical elements in the feminist movement unjustifiably hinders women in ministry. I've discovered, that a major factor in not accepting women as pastors for many persons is that they have been turned off by stereotyping all feminists on the basis of a few vocal spokespersons. They are prejudiced against feminists because they wrongly believe that feminism necessarily and always advances a non-biblical agenda. When describing myself, I say that I believe in biblical equality as it is affirmed in the first and second chapters of Genesis and Galatians 3:28. Advancing women in ministry is not a feminist issue; it's a biblical issue.

The Biblical Holiness Movement Teaching of Gender Equality Predates Feminism

In your letter, you suggested that my desire to advance women in ministry is "a modern feminist thing." Actually, the reverse is true. The first wave of

North American feminism has its roots in biblically-based holiness Christianity. Holiness Christianity and abolitionism formed the foundation of feminism. As abolitionists made a biblical case to release the slaves, they frequently referred to Galatians 3:28, "There is no longer Jew or Greek, there is no longer slave or free, there is no longer male and female; for all of you are one in Christ Jesus." Cowles wrote, "Galatians 3:28 became the Magna Carta text for Evangelicals advocating the abolition of slavery, as well as the enfranchisement of women" (1993:116). As preachers stumped for abolitionism, they increasingly recognized that their arguments applied also to women.

Most holiness churches have always made a place for women in leadership. C. S. Cowles writes: "From their various beginnings, holiness churches in the Wesleyan-Arminian tradition have granted women all of the rights and privileges of membership, ministry, and leadership that are accorded to men" (1993:21). These holiness churches, such as The Salvation Army, Church of God (Anderson), and Church of the Nazarene predate modern feminism. Stan Ingersol adds, "A century ago the holiness tradition was in the forefront of women's ordination" (1994:632.) Susie Stanley notes, "For the most part, Wesleyan/Holiness denominations issued licenses and ordination papers regardless of sex" (2002:106), adding, "Committed to egalitarian primitivism, the Wesleyan/Holiness movement emulated the early church by validating the prophetic authority of women" (2002:211). John Wesley did not embrace the call of women early in his ministry but warmed up to it as his ministry progressed. Catherine Booth notes that, "From the Methodist Conference, held at Manchester, 1787, Mr. Wesley wrote to Miss Sarah Mallett, whose labours, while very acceptable to the people, had been opposed by some of the preachers: 'We give the right hand of fellowship to Sarah Mallett, and have no objection to her being a preacher in our connection, so long as she preaches Methodist doctrine, and attends to our discipline' " (1859:19). In 1835 Oberlin College in Ohio became the first college to admit women. This was a biblical stand. In 1848 Elizabeth Cady Stanton organized the first women's rights convention at a Wesleyan chapel in Seneca Falls, New York, where they drafted the Declaration of Sentiments. As John Stanley notes, "The Salvation Army released this statement in 1879:

> Section XII. Female Preachers—As it is manifest from the Scripture of the Old and especially the New Testament that God has sanctioned the labors of Godly women in His Church; Godly women possessing the necessary gifts and

qualifications, shall be employed as preachers itinerant or otherwise and class leaders and as such shall have appointments given to them on the preachers plan; and they shall be eligible for any office, and to speak and vote at all official meetings" (1999:49).

In 1872, though women still did not have the right to vote, Victoria Woodhull ran for President. John Stanley records that, in 1899, "Members of the General Council of the New Testament Church of Christ, a forerunner of the Church of the Nazarene 'decided that under the gospel women had all the rights and privileges that men enjoy. Since there is neither Jew nor Greek, bond or free, male nor female in Christ, a woman is eligible for ordination'" (1999:49). Stanley records that in 1920 F. G. Smith, a key leader in the Church of God (Anderson), wrote an editorial to *The Gospel Trumpet*:

> Again, I call your attention to the organization of the church by the Holy Spirit. A man is an evangelist because he has the gift of evangelizing. It is not because he is a man, but because he has that particular gift. The gift itself is the proof of his calling. If a woman has divine gifts fitting her for a particular work in the church, that is the proof, and the only proof needed, that that is her place. Any other basis of qualification is than divine gifts is superficial and arbitrary and ignores the divine plan of organization and government in the church (1999:50).

The first wave of feminism began in Holiness churches as they grappled with biblical truth. The push for equality for women gained momentum from abolitionism. It reached its crescendo in 1920 as women finally won the right to vote in the United States.

Second Wave or modern feminism was born in the 1960s. This is the feminism that is frequently stereotyped as embracing a non-biblical social agenda. The National Organization for Women (NOW) was created in New York in 1966. This organization contains feminists both with and without a biblical worldview. We rightly disassociate ourselves from ungodly and unbiblical views; there is nothing, however, unbiblical about the equality of women and men. There is still a great need for caring persons to work for gender equality. Today, women pastor only 6 percent of Church of God (Anderson) congregations (Hawkins, 2002:2). This inequality falls far short of Paul's magnificent statement of non-discrimination in Galatians 3:28, "There is no longer Jew or Greek, there is no longer slave or free, there is no longer male and female; for all of you are one in Christ Jesus."

Dr. Chang, my desire to advance women in ministry is not "a modern feminist thing." I am standing on biblical truth that holiness churches have continuously affirmed long before modern feminism even began. I hope that this has clarified my position. I would be happy to explore with you the biblical references that affirm gender equality. I firmly believe that God calls and equips women to be leaders at all levels in the church. May God bless you. I look forward to hearing from you.

Sincerely,

Reverend Randal Huber

Discussion Questions for Chapter 8

1. The author affirms that some persons may be resistant to women pastors in part because they are reacting to stereotypes of modern feminism? What do you think?

2. Is it important for those who believe in biblical equality to disassociate from non-biblical elements in feminism? Why or why not?

3. Some believe that those who affirm biblical equality are following modern feminism instead of the Bible. Why is it significant that the Holiness churches, that have historically affirmed biblical equality, predate modern feminism?

4. In what ways are women still treated as second-class persons in the church and society?

5. Why is it important to continue affirming biblical equality in the church and society?

6. Should changing the second-class treatment of women be a priority for the church? Why or why not?

A Sin Against God

Chapter 9

Dear Randy:

When I heard your testimony the Lord put me under conviction. Like you, I have pastored for many years in a movement that has allowed women pastors from the beginning. I truthfully believe women should be pastors. What I have just realized is that I have been doing basically nothing to advance the placement of women pastors. I have been committing a sin against God by failing to do everything in my power to correct the injustices in the church. I've been apathetic. I humbly repent. I want to live out Galatians 3:28. "There is no longer Jew or Greek, there is no longer slave or free, there is no longer male and female; for all of you are one in Christ Jesus." I need some guidance. How can I best minister to the injustice and pain of my Christian sisters and what can I do to help?

Thanks for sharing with me. I'm a changed man.

Peace,

Antoine

Dear Antoine,

I praise God for your responsiveness to the Holy Spirit. For several years I believed that God called and equipped women to be pastors but I did little or nothing to help their cause. Like you, I had to repent. Since 1995, I have labored to help the church to recognize how important this issue is. Here are some specific ways that you can help.

Share the Biblical and Historical Case for Women in Ministry.

As a pastor you have the unique opportunity of regularly sharing with your congregation what the Bible affirms about women in ministry. By doing so, you are affirming what your movement has always believed. In the earlier years of my ministry, I was reticent to teach about women in ministry because I knew some in my congregation did not agree with me. On reflection, I realize I was more concerned with the opinions of human beings than with affirming the truths of God's word. As pastors and church leaders, we are responsible to teach the whole counsel of scripture. We must lovingly preach the truth, even when it is unpopular with some in our congregations.

We must also be willing "to speak the truth in love" to those who express prejudice against women. We need to consistently uphold the biblical equality of men and women. We need to help our Christian brothers and sisters to understand that prejudice against women is a sin against God. God created every man and woman in the divine image. Jesus died for men and for women. The Holy Spirit gifts both men and women. God calls and equips both men and women. I'm not advocating vain arguments and worthless polemics, but I am affirming that we need to labor faithfully in helping others to see the value of those women who carry on the leadership heritages of Miriam, Deborah, Huldah, Anna, Mary, Lydia, Phoebe, Priscilla, and Junia. I am advocating that we create a tone in our congregation that accepts and respects the contributions of women leaders in our midst.

We must be willing to confront faulty theology. I have heard some make this argument. "If God is truly calling a woman to be a pastor, then God will prepare a church to call that woman as their pastor." The unfortunate corollary to that statement is, "If a woman can't find a church to pastor, then God must not be calling her." This statement leans heavily upon the sovereignty of God but fails to give adequate responsibility to the people God has called to be the church. God may indeed be leading a congregation to call a woman pastor but that congregation may be disobedient. Sometimes things that God desires do not come to pass because of human sin. For example, the Bible clearly states that God is not willing that any should perish but that all should come to eternal life (2 Pet 3:9). The sad reality is that "broad is the way that leads to destruction and narrow is the path that leads to eternal life and there are few that find it" (Matt 7:13–14). How can God's desire that none shall perish fail to happen? Some who hear the gospel choose to reject Christ. Some who are called to make disciples fail to witness. Some women who are called to preach are hindered by the church from fulfilling their calling. As believers, we are responsible to be obedient to the Lord. Good theology acknowledges both the sovereignty of God and human responsibility to be obedient to the Lord.

We need to help congregations that have little or no experience with female leaders to begin to understand the possibilities. Marilyn Henry notes, "The first problem to overcome is that most congregations have simply never thought of having a female minister" (1980:9). We can invite female preachers to preach in our pulpits. We can quote female pastors in our sermons. We can use examples of female leaders in our preaching and teaching. We can affirm the roles of female pastors and leaders in our heritage. We stand on scripture and heritage. The church has a need for godly leaders. D. Elton Trueblood wrote, "If in our contemporary thinking, we combine our beginnings, our history, and our present predicament, we come out with a clear conclusion. Women belong to the Christian faith and we need to take the fullest possible advantage of their potential contribution now!" (1980:3).

Share the Facts about Placement of Women Pastors in the Church of God

The facts indicate signs of hope but also a long way to go. Juanita Leonard notes the highest percentage of Church of God congregations pastored by women was 32 percent in 1925 (1989:175). In 1985, women pastored only two percent of Church of God congregations. (1989:175). Since 1985 there has been an improvement. Mary Ann Hawkins, in her Fuller Theological Seminary comprehensive exam, notes that women pastor 6 percent of the 2232 congregations of the Church of God (2002:2). The *2002 Yearbook of the Church of God* lists 7,469 ministers, 1,583 of which are women. Women represent approximately 21 percent of this total. Hawkins' research also indicates that 182 women are classified as senior or solo pastors.[12] This represents 2.43 percent of all ministers registered in the *2002 Yearbook of the Church of God*. In addition, Hawkins' research indicates that 566 women are classified as associate pastors (2002:2–3). This represents 7.57 percent of ministers listed in the yearbook.[13] The combined total of women pastors and associate pastors is 748. This number represents 10 percent of all ministers listed in the *2002 Yearbook of the Church of God*.

Let me summarize: Twenty-one percent of all ministers listed in the *2002 Yearbook of the Church of God* are women. Women pastors and associate pastors combined represent 10 percent of all ministers in the Church of God. Women pastor 6 percent of all Church of God congregations. Since women represent at least 50 percent of the constituency of the Church of God, women are clearly under-represented as ministers, pastors and associate pastors in the church. Why has the percentage of congregations pastored by women dropped from 32 percent in 1925 to 6 percent in 2002?[14]

Many factors are responsible. Susie Stanley suggests that as the Church of God developed, it moved away from prophetic leadership to priestly leadership. In the early years of the Church of God, women pastors were welcomed on the basis of prophetic authority but as itinerant ministry diminished and settled into congregational life, women lost a key outlet for ministry (1996:149). A young movement was more inclined to accept women pastors than a more developed movement. Stanley adds, "While most Wesleyan/Holiness churches ordained women from their inceptions, for the most part, they have yet to concede priestly authority to women at the highest institutional levels" (1996:149). This is identified by Stanley as "...the acquiescence to cultural stereotypes that support males in leadership roles and limit women's participation in positions of authority" (1996:150). Hawkins adds, "The culture has significant impact upon what a woman perceives she may do, or is expected to do" (2002:3). As the church has continued to accept patriarchy uncritically while simultaneously moving toward a more settled congregational life, women have been discouraged from leadership. Buttressing this position is what Paul Bassett has termed "fundamentalist leavening" (1978: 65–91). Susie Stanley writes of this term.

> Often theological justification has been utilized to support cultural stereotypes. Fundamentalists who oppose the leadership of women in the church attempt to support their position by keeping alive the arguments derived from 1 Timothy 2 and 1 Corinthians 14, insisting on a literal interpretation of these passages of scripture (1996:150).

Cowles is more strident: "… Isolated verses have been ripped out of context and used as clubs to bludgeon women back into their traditional status of subservience, submissiveness, and silence" (1993:177). Many in Church of God congregations, ignorant of their holiness roots that accepted the prophetic role of women pastors, have adopted the theological position of media attractive fundamentalism. This was the mind-set that I encountered at Chapel Hill Church of God in York Springs, Pennsylvania, from 1982–1995. Our congregation was initially founded by women leaders and historically accepted female leadership, but in a period of pastoral vacancy was greatly influenced by fundamentalism and changed the bylaws to exclude women from leadership. It took years to help this congregation to reclaim its holiness and biblical roots. While many congregations have never changed their bylaws to prohibit women from leadership, the practices in those same congregations exclude women.

Women considering a call to ministry face an uphill challenge. Sometimes their own families, pastors, or congregations discourage them on theological grounds. Sometimes their families, pastors, or congregations dishearten them on the basis that they will be committing themselves to years of expensive education and preparation and then have great difficulty in finding placement. Some women give up. Some leave the Church of God when they cannot find a place to exercise their spiritual gifts.

Sadly, placement problems for women are a reality for women in the Church of God. In her *History of Women in Leadership,* Hawkins notes that her research indicates that gender bias has adversely affected women in ministry in the Church of God (2002:2). In addition to her survey research, Hawkins interviewed six clergywomen in depth. She writes, "Each of these clergywomen, at least once (and several multiple times) has been rejected for positional ministry within the Church of God on the basis of gender alone" (2002:2).

I add to this research my own recently completed research with licensed and ordained female ministers exploring their attitudes toward ministry placement in the Church of God.[15] I sent surveys to 1127 licensed and ordained women in the Church of God (Appendix A).[16] 241 women returned surveys. This represents a response rate of 21 percent. In the surveys I used a rating scale of 1 = strongly agree, 2 = agree, 3 = undecided, 4 = disagree, and 5 = strongly disagree. When one averages the answers to all of the questions, the respondents' attitude toward their placement in the Church of God was undecided (Appendix B). According to the raw numbers, some women are genuinely satisfied with their placement experiences. Others are dissatisfied.

For me, the most helpful question in my survey is number 8. Question 8 states, "My female gender has had no significant impact upon my ministerial placement in the Church of God." Two hundred and four women answered this question. Thirty-three strongly agreed, fifty-two agreed, twenty-six undecided, fifty-nine disagreed, thirty-four strongly disagreed. The average response was 3.04. 45.6 percent of respondents disagreed with this statement. In other words, nearly half of the respondents believe that their gender has impacted their placement experiences. Consider the implications. All over North America there are women who have responded to God's call to lead the church but sexist prejudice is impacting their opportunities to use their spiritual gifts. Both they and the church are impoverished. There is great room for improvement.

Provide Support and Advocacy to Women in Ministry.

Antoine, I believe all Christians have the responsibility of affirming those God is calling into ministry. I'm not sure we do a great job, even with men, but women need even more affirmation because of the extra obstacles and prejudices that they face. I will be forever grateful for the kind and generous support that my childhood priest and congregation extended to me as I considered full-time Christian service. I owe a great debt to Rev. Leslie Harding and the Episcopal Church of the Holy Cross. Most Christian leaders I know can look back with gratitude to those who encouraged them in their calling. Men and women entering ministry need advocates who will provide spiritual, emotional, and sometimes even financial support. When you know a man or woman considering a call to a particular congregation, contact that congregation to let them know of the gifts, maturity, and character of that person. Step out and help that congregation to clearly appreciate that person's capabilities. Be like John the Baptist who prepares the way for ministry.

While many women are satisfied with their calling and their placement in the church, we must recognize the additional burdens that women in ministry face. Some have regularly experienced doors closing in their faces because of gender. Some have been marginalized, rejected, and ignored. Arlo Newell, former editor of *Vital Christianity*, wrote: "Rejection can be non-verbal—no outspoken opposition at all—only isolation, exclusion from full participation in key leadership roles" (1989:12).

Let me share some quotations that women wrote in the "comments" section of the surveys that I sent to licensed and ordained Church of God female ministers in 2002–2003 (Appendix A).

- One retired minister wrote: "I am keenly aware that many of the younger women are having difficulties and the church as a whole must address the issues."

- A minister who is serving part-time and who has sought pastoral placement in the Church of God within the last five years wrote: "When reading the church report on vacancies, they're saying how short of evangelists and pastors the Church of God [is]. [But] you are never contacted. What good did it do us to supply this data? They pick and choose." On her survey, this minister strongly disagreed with the statement, "My female gender has had no significant impact upon my ministerial placement in the Church of God."
- One forty-one to fifty year old minister wrote: "Women ministers in Alabama Church of God are not respected as women servants of God. They are not qualified to be pastors, only preachers and that's wrong."
- An African-American fifty-one to sixty year old minister currently seeking placement wrote: "I would welcome even an opportunity or invitation to preach at any Church of God congregation—period. I am very disillusioned with the Church of God and it's lack of love and unity."
- A Caucasian woman with a bachelors degree who strongly agreed with the statement, "I am called to professional ministry, but I have been unable to find a position in the Church of God commensurate with my education and gifts" wrote "I put in full-time hours (30 or more a week) but I am unpaid; I have a financial support that allows me to do that."
- A Caucasian part-time associate pastor commented, "Although an ordained seminary grad they refuse to call me an Associate pastor, or even Minister of Music—I'm the 'Choir Director.'"
- A fifty-one to sixty year old Caucasian minister with a Masters degree who is currently seeking placement wrote: "I find there is nearly no opportunity to serve as a full-time (or even part-time) associate in pastoral care in the Church of God. Nearly every associate pastor position is for music or youth. I am called and prepared to serve but still wait. Meanwhile, I earn a living elsewhere and minister wherever possible as a lay-person. P.S. Other churches ... are interested. Still I wait on Church of God placement."
- An African-American minister who has sought placement in the

Church of God within the last five years and who strongly disagreed with the statement, "A mentor or church leader has advocated for me to assist in finding placement," wrote: "It seems the male pastors do little to encourage female ministers to seek pastorates. There is very little mentoring in this regard and very, very, very little encouragement to seek pastorates. They want you to work, serve on committees, yes—but seek full-time pastorates, NO!"

- Another African-American minister with a Masters degree from a non-Church of God institution, who has sought placement in the Church of God within the last five years and who is currently serving as a ministry volunteer, wrote: "The Church of God has no structural system for placing people. Males are highly favored in the local church scene. There is no help but to wait on the Lord to open doors."

It hurts to be prepared spiritually and academically but to see no placement on the horizon.

Antoine, provide personal and prayer support for your Christian sisters. Walk with them and advocate for them.

Hold Church Leaders Accountable to Advance Women in Ministry

Most church leaders in Wesleyan/Holiness churches say they believe in women in ministry. The trouble is that many do little or nothing to actually advance the placement of women pastors. We don't want to confront confused biblical teaching because we fear we might drive some people out of our congregations. We don't want to confront centuries of patriarchy and prejudice against women. We put higher priorities on other things. We don't want to "make waves."

I had to repent and you are now repenting. We have realized it is not enough to talk the talk. We need to walk the walk. Richard Goode wrote, "We need a national repentance among men for the unfair biases we have held toward women, especially those seeking to pastor" (1989:21). We need to hold our leaders accountable to practice what they preach. Church leaders need to affirm and actively advocate for women in ministry. When congregations are resistant to female leadership, our leaders must be held accountable to teach these congregations the biblical and historical basis for women pastors. Sometimes, we need to remind our leaders about the need to prepare congregations to receive women in ministry. We who lead must be held accountable to put God's word into practice.

Call the Church to Repent of the Sin of Sexism.

I believe that most persons in the church who are doing little to advance women in ministry are not deliberately sexist. They did not wake up one morning and decide, "I'm going to be against women in ministry. I'm going to keep women down." Sexism, like racism, enters our values imperceptibly. We fail to value and advance women in leadership because human culture is largely patriarchal. Men are typically in charge. Women are typically marginalized. Edward C. Lehman writes the following analysis: "The major culprit in this pattern is not conscious and malicious sexism. Rather it is the latent institutionalized assumptions about the nature of God, the Church, and its traditions that repeatedly call members back from the brink of experimentation and change" (1987:326). We are hesitant to change those things that have become the basic fabric of our lives.

As I look back on my own life, I recognize many sexist elements that I just "caught" from my religious background and my prevailing culture. I can make similar claims about racism. I have spent years repenting of racist elements in my upbringing. Now I am pressing toward holiness by seeking full reconciliation with all of my Christian brothers and sisters. Many can see similar cultural and institutionalized influences in their own lives. Our racism or sexism may not have been deliberately chosen but racism is still sin. Sexism is still sin. We need to repent of both. Both hinder the work of God. Both fall far below God's perfect will for the church. It is a sin for the church to persist in allowing women to be the group most discriminated against in virtually every culture, civilization, and race. Change is hard, but that is no excuse for doing little or nothing. It is sin if the church persists in allowing women to be relegated to second-class status and refuses to allow them the full use of their God given spiritual gifts. It is sin when women are disqualified from ministry because the church, disregarding the full counsel of scripture, clings stubbornly to a couple of poorly exegeted biblical texts for support of sexism. It is sin to know the truth and to do little or nothing to apply it to our own lives, congregations, movements, and denominations. Miles affirms, "Our message is simple and so clear that it cannot be denied. Every revolution in the history of the world, every movement for equality, has stopped short of sexual equality. After thousands of years, this era has made a start on changing that. Let us not rest until all of us are free" (2001:14).

Antoine, I deeply appreciate your willingness to get more involved in advancing the placement of women pastors. I pray that others will see as you have seen and respond in passionate obedience to the Lord. We can make a difference. Standing on scripture and faithful to our heritage, the Holy Spirit will bless our efforts. God does not intend for anyone to be second-class in the kingdom. God calls and equips males and females to pastor. Here is the truth we Christians proclaim. Here is the truth we must live. "There is no longer Jew or Greek, there is no longer slave or free, there is no longer male and female; for all of you are one in Christ Jesus (Gal 3:28, NRSV). It's time to embrace the complete equality of all believers. It's time to reclaim our biblical and historical heritage. May we press on to full maturity in Christ. May we not rest until every called and equipped woman finds her place in ministry.

In Christian Love,

Randy Huber

Discussion Questions for Chapter 9

1. How are sexism and racism similar?

2. Why are sexism and racism sins against God?

3. What is your reaction to the placement of women pastors statistics in the Church of God?

4. What are some tangible ways that you can support and advocate for a woman seeking to pastor?

5. How can you hold Christian leaders accountable to labor against the sin of sexism?

6. How can a congregation prepare itself to be receptive to women in leadership?

7. What insights have you gained from studying this book?

8. What action steps will you take as a result of studying this book?

END NOTES

1. According to Louie Crew, "in 1973, there were no women priests." "Women now constitute 13.8 percent of those listed in the 1998 *Episcopal Clerical Directory"* (2002:1).
2. Lima Lehmer Williams served in Kenya from 1936–1961. She wrote: *Walking in Missionary Shoes:* (1905–1970) *A History of the Church of God in East Africa.* Anderson, Ind: Warner Press. 1986.
3. All Dana Brown quotations are from correspondence to me dated December 3, 2002.
4. All Mary Ann Hawkins direct quotations are taken from correspondence to me dated December 13, 2002.
5. Carolyn Waddy Reid and her husband Noah W. Reid Jr. currently co-pastor Langley Avenue Church of God in Chicago, Illinois.
6. All quotations of Mandy Stanley are from correspondence with me in December 2002.
7. All Barbara O. Berry quotations are from correspondence with me dated January 9, 2003.
8. All quotations of Barbara Deale Miller are taken from correspondence to me dated November 2, 2002.
9. All Cheryl Sanders quotations are taken from correspondence with me dated March 11, 2003.
10. All Rita Johnson quotations are taken from correspondence with me dated December 10, 2002.
11. Charles W. Naylor, "The Church's Jubilee" *Worship the Lord: Hymnal of the Church of God* (Anderson, Ind: Warner Press, 1989), 312.
12. These 182 women include the categories senior pastor, primary pastor, co-pastor, pastor/evangelist, church planter, and interim pastor (2002:2).

END NOTES

13. These categories include: non-licensed associate, interim associate pastor, associate pastor, and associates of administration, evangelism, assimilation, business administration, counseling, children's ministry, discipleship, family life, Christian education, music, and visitation (2002:2–3).

14. I speculate that a concerted effort of the Church of God, begun in 1989, positively impacted the rise from 2 percent of Church of God congregations pastored by women in 1985 to 6 percent in 2002. This effort included Juanita Leonard's book *Called to Minister, Empowered to Serve* and a substantial focus on women in ministry in the May 1989 issue of *Vital Christianity,* the official publication of the Church of God. This effort to educate the church has continued as many key educators, pastors, and leaders in the Church of God have labored continuously to raise the awareness of the church to return to its biblical and historical roots.

15. My doctoral dissertation, *Advancing the Placement of Women Pastors in the Church of God,* contains all of my research and is available at the Nicholson Library of Anderson University, Anderson, Indiana.

16. This figure represents all licensed and ordained women listed in the *2002 Yearbook of the Church of God.* I sent surveys only to licensed and ordained women because they are the most likely women to be affected by placement issues in the church.

Selected Bibliography

From time to time you will find statements that end in parentheses that look like this (2000:58). The numbers represent the publication date "2000" and page number "58" of the work being cited. The author's name is cited in the text. To view the source turn to the Selected Bibliography in the back of the book. Find the author's name. The authors are listed alphabetically. Find the publishing date under the author's name. That is the source quoted. In addition, you will find Endnotes listed at the back of the book.

ALLISON, JOSEPH

1978   "An Overview of the Involvement of Women in the Church of God from 1916." *The Role of Women in Today's World.* Anderson, Ind: Commission on Social Concerns, Church of God. Allison writes a brief overview of women ministers in the Church of God, spanning six decades. He covers women evangelists, pastors, home missionaries, foreign missionaries, as well as social changes affecting women in ministry.

BASSETT, PAUL MERRITT

1978   "The Fundamentalist Leavening of the Holiness Movement, 1914–1940: The Church of the Nazarene—A Case Study." *Wesleyan Theological Journal 13,* no 1. This article explores the impact of fundamentalism on the question of biblical authority and inspiration and other theological positions in the Church of the Nazarene.

SELECTED BIBLIOGRAPHY

BAUMGARDNER, JENNIFER and RICHARDS, AMY

    2000   *Manifesta: Young Women, Feminism, and the Future.* New York: Farrar, Straus and Giroux. A secular work by "Third Wave Feminists," the authors access the history, current status, and direction of feminism.

BECKER, CAROL E.

    1993   "Women in Church Leadership: An Emerging Paradigm." *Leading the Congregation.* Norman Shawchuck and Roger Heuser, General Editors. Nashville: Abingdon Press. The author explores how women leaders are impacting the church.

BILEZIKIAN, GILBERT

    1985   *Beyond Sex Roles: What the Bible Says About a Woman's Place in Church and Family.* Grand Rapids: Baker Book House. An outstanding resource, Bilezikian elucidates helpful and cogent biblical arguments concerning women's roles.

BOOTH, CATHERINE

    1859   *Female Ministry: or Women's Right to Preach the Gospel.* 1975 Reprint. New York: Salvation Army Supplies Printing and Publishing Department. Booth presents a classic, relevant, and concise argument for women in ministry.

CALLEN, BARRY

    1992   *She Came Preaching: The Life and Ministry of Lillie S. McCutcheon.* Anderson, Ind: Warner Press. Callen writes an interesting and informative biography on one of the great leaders of the Church of God.

    1992   *Thinking and Acting Together.* Anderson, IN: Executive Council of the Church of God and Warner Press. Callen compiles key decisions and resolutions made by the General Assembly of the Church of God. Of particular interest is the June 1974 resolution found on page 66.

CARMODY, DENISE LARDNER

1988 *Biblical Woman: Contemporary Reflections on Scriptural Texts.* New York: The Crossroad Publishing Company. Carmody explores twenty-four key biblical texts, considering the impact upon contemporary women.

CLARKE, ADAM

1825 *The Holy Bible Containing the Old and New Testaments with A Commentary and Critical Notes: The Old Testament Volume III.* Nashville: Abingdon.

COLESON, JOSEPH E.

1996 *Ezer Cenegdo: A Power Like Him, Facing Him as Equal.* Grantham, Penn: Wesleyan/Holiness Women Clergy. Coleson puts forth an effective exposition reflecting upon the meaning of "helper" in the Genesis account.

COWLES, C. S.

1993 *A Woman's Place? Leadership in the Church.* Kansas City: Beacon Hill Press of Kansas City. An outstanding resource, Cowles has written one of the clearest, most comprehensive, and best-reasoned arguments for women in ministry available today.

CREW, LOUIE

2002 *Female Priests in the Episcopal Church.* Rutgers University: http://newark.rutgers.edu/~lcrew/womenpr.html

DAYTON, DONALD WILBER, ed.

1993 *Holiness Tracts Defending the Ministry of Women.* New York: Garland Publishing, Inc. A valuable resource, this book contains three rare nineteenth century and one early twentieth century tract defending women in ministry. The contributors are Luther Lee, B. T. Roberts, Catherine Booth, and Fannie McDowell Hunter.

Selected Bibliography

DEEN, EDITH

1959 *Great Women of the Christian Faith.* Chappaqua, NY: Christian Herald Books. This older work includes 121 biographies of Christian women spanning nineteen centuries. This work is adversely impacted by 1950s stereotypes.

EDWARDS, RUTH B.

1989 *The Case For Women's Ministry.* London: SPCK. Edwards presents reasoned, biblical arguments for and against women in ministry. She writes from an Episcopalian perspective.

ELDRED, JOHN O.

1981 *Women Pastors: If God Calls, Why Not the Church?* Valley Forge, Penn: Judson Press. Eldred explores some of the reasons that the church has difficulty accepting women pastors. Among these reasons are: the question of competency, problems accepting change, gender competition, theology, resentment, human sexuality, marital status, and honesty.

ERICKSON-PEARSON, JAN

1980 "But YOU Can't be a Pastor." *Centering on Ministry.* Winter 1980 Volume 5, Number 2, Anderson, Ind: The Center For Pastoral Studies Anderson College School of Theology. This brief article is a testimonial of Erickson-Pearson's self-understandings and struggles in pursuing her call to ministry.

EVANS, MARY J.

1983 *Woman in the Bible.* Downers Grove, Ill: InterVarsity Press. Supporting women in ministry and utilizing careful exegesis, Evans explores the relevant Old and New Testament texts that concern women in ministry.

FITZWATER, P. B.

1949 *Woman (Her Mission, Position, and Ministry).* Grand Rapids: Eerdmans.

GOODE, RICHARD

1989   "A Tragic Question: Should Women Become Pastors?" *Vital Christianity*. May 1989. In this brief article, Goode laments that the Church of God, whose historical stand has been for women in ministry, should even need to ask whether women should be pastors.

GRENZ, STANLEY and KHESBO, and MUIR, DENISE

1995   *Women in the Church: A Biblical Theology of Women in Ministry*. Downers Grove, Ill: InterVarsity Press. The Grenz's and Muir explore the Bible's teachings concerning women in ministry.

GROOTHUIS, REBECCA MERRILL

1997   *Good News For Women: A Biblical Picture of Gender Equality*. Grand Rapids: Baker Books. Groothuis puts forth a helpful and biblical view of gender equality.

GRUBBS, JERRY C.

1980   "Women in Ministry: An Introduction to This Issue." *Centering on Ministry*. Winter 1980 Volume 5, Number 2, Anderson, Ind: The Center For Pastoral Studies Anderson College School of Theology. Grubbs briefly examines seventy years of statistics and asks whether the Church of God is currently open to women pastors.

HARKNESS, GEORGIA

1972   *Women in Church and Society*. Nashville: Abingdon Press. An insightful reflection about women's roles.

HAWKINS, MARY ANN

2002   *Women Clergy in the Church of God Today: A Dissertation Tutorial Presented to the Faculty of the School of World Mission and Institute of Church Growth*. Fuller Theological Seminary, "In Partial Fulfillment of the Requirements for the Degree of Doctor of Philosophy." Hawkins has compiled the most recent and complete data available on women clergy in the Church of God.

2002 *History of Women in Leadership.* Unpublished Comprehensive Examination written for the faculty of the School of World Mission and Institute of Church Growth. Fuller Theological Seminary, "In Partial Fulfillment of the Requirements for the Degree of Doctor of Philosophy." Available electronically from the author at mah@qwestinternet.net. Hawkins explores the causes of the difference between the Church of God position on women in ministry and the actual numbers of women pastors in the Church of God.

HAYES, RICHARD B.

1996 *Moral Vision of the New Testament.* San Francisco: HarperSanFrancisco, Hayes considers selected Pauline scriptures that inform the issue of women in ministry.

HENRY, MARILYN K.

1980 "A Personal Perspective on Women in Ministry." *Centering on Ministry.* Winter 1980 Volume 5, Number 2, Anderson, Ind: The Center For Pastoral Studies Anderson College School of Theology. Henry presents a brief personal testimonial.

HILLMAN, CASSIE

2000 "Women in Ministry: A Historical and Moral Reflection." An unpublished paper written for a class taught by Dr. James W. Lewis at Anderson University, Anderson, Indiana. Available electronically from the author at Kansas_@hotmail.com. Utilizing historical resources and research from e-mail correspondence with leaders in the Church of God, Hillman explores opposition to women in ministry in the Church of God.

HUBER, RANDY and STANLEY, JOHN

1999 *Reclaiming the Wesleyan/Holiness Heritage of Women Clergy: Sermons, A Case Study and Resources.* Grantham, Penn: Wesleyan/Holiness Women Clergy c/o of Messiah College. This booklet contains eleven sermons on women in ministry, a case study for change at the local level, and selected resources.

HULL, GRETCHEN GAEBELEIN

1987   *Equal to Serve: Men and Women Working Together Revealing the Gospel.* Grand Rapids: Baker Books.

1995   *Empowered to Serve.* www.cbeinternational.org/new/free_articles/empowered_to serve.html.

INGERSOL, STAN

1994   "Holiness Women." *Christian Century.* June 29–July 6, 1994 Volume 3. A brief survey of holiness women.

JEWETT, PAUL K.

1980   *Ordination of Women.* Grand Rapids: William B. Eerdmans. Jewett explores the question of ordaining women. He utilizes the format of argument followed by response. He concludes favoring the ordination of women.

KEENER, CRAIG S.

1992   *The IVP Bible Background Commentary.* Downers Grove, Ill: InterVarsity Press.

KROEGER, RICHARD and CLARK, CATHERINE

1992   *I Suffer Not a Woman: Rethinking 1 Timothy 2:11–15 in Light of Ancient Evidence.* Grand Rapids: Baker Books. The Kroegers write extensively and in depth about the Ephesian context of 1 Timothy 2:11–15, shedding unique light upon 1 Timothy 2:11–15.

Toward an Egalitarian Hermeneutic of Faith. Found on the Christians for Biblical Equality Web page www.cbeinternational.org/new/free_articles/egalitarian_hermene utic.html. This brief article argues for an egalitarian understanding of gender in scripture.

SELECTED BIBLIOGRAPHY

LAIRD, REBECCA

1992   *Ordained Women in the Church of the Nazarene: The First Generation.* Kansas City, Mo: Nazarene Publishing House. Laird tells the stories of a dozen early ministers in the Church of the Nazarene and explores the issue of women in ministry from the nineteenth century to the present.

LAYMAN, FRED D.

1980   "Male Headship in Paul's Thought." *Wesleyan Theological Journal.* Volume 15 Number 1, Spring 1980. This scholarly article critically explores the meaning of headship in Paul's writing.

LEE, LUTHER

1975   "Women's Right to Preach the Gospel. A Sermon, Preached at the Ordination of The Rev. Miss Antoinette L. Brown at South Butler, Wayne County, NY, Sept. 15, 1853" *Five Sermons and a Tract.* Edited by Donald W. Dayton. Chicago: Holrad House. This nineteenth century sermon presents clear biblical arguments for women in ministry.

LEHMAN, EDWARD C.

1987   "Research on Lay Church Members Attitudes Toward Women Clergy: An Assessment." *Review of Religious Literature.* Volume 28 No. 4 June 1987, Brockport: State University of New York.

LEONARD, JUANITA EVANS, ed.

1989   *Called to Minister: Empowered to Serve.* Anderson, Ind: Warner Press. This book of essays written by Church of God leaders is a must read for all who are interested in the subject of women in ministry in the Church of God. It comprehensively covers biblical, historical, ethical, and statistical issues that impact the issue of women in ministry in the Church of God.

1989   *Church of God Women in Ministry Through the Last Century.* Anderson, Ind: Prepared for Women in Ministry and Missions June 1989. This resource is an alphabetical listing of the ordination years for women in ministry in the Church of God from the turn of the twentieth century through 1989. An addendum is available bringing the list forward to 1995.

LOCKYER, HERBERT

1967   *The Women of the Bible.* Grand Rapids: Zondervan. This earlier work explores the lives of various biblical women.

LONGENECKER, RICHARD N.

1984   *New Testament Social Ethics For Today.* Grand Rapids: William B. Eerdmans.

MAXWELL, L. E.

1987   *Women in Ministry.* Camp Hill, Penn: Christian Publications. Maxwell explores the Bible and history considering the roles of women in Christian leadership. Maxwell explores some key biblical texts.

MAY, GRACE YING and JOE, HYUNHYE POKRIFKA

1998   "Priscilla Papers, Setting the Record Straight: A Response to J. I. Packer's Position on Women's Ordination." *Priscilla Papers* edited by Gretchen Gabelein Hull. Volume 11, Number 1, Winter. Web version www.cbeinternational.org/new/free_articles/may.html.

McCUTCHEON, LILLIE S.

1980   "Lady in the Pulpit." *Centering on Ministry.* Winter 1980, Volume 5, Number 2, Anderson, Ind: The Center For Pastoral Studies Anderson College School of Theology. McCutcheon pens a brief article elucidating her perspective on being a woman minister. She includes brief advice for other women pastors.

1989   "God is an Equal Opportunity Employer." *Vital Christianity.* May 1989. This short article is McCutcheon's appeal for women in ministry.

MICKELSEN, ALVERA, ed.

1985 *Women, Authority & the Bible.* Downers Grove, Ill: InterVarsity Press. A helpful resource, this collection of essays includes a collection of twenty-one Christian scholars' arguments for and against women in ministry.

MILLER, ADAM W.

1978 "Principles of Interpretation Related to the Social Teachings of Paul." *The Role of Women in Today's World.* Anderson, Ind: Commission on Social Concerns, Church of God. Miller explores hermeneutical principles that affect Paul's treatment of women.

MILES, ROSALIND

1988 *Who Cooked the Last Supper? The Women's History of the World.* New York: Three Rivers Press. This secular work explores the contributions and impact of scores of females throughout the history of the world. While the worldview is neither biblical nor Christian, Miles presents the stories of numerous overlooked and forgotten women who have impacted world history.

MITCHELL, ELLA PEARSON

1991 *Women to Preach or not to Preach.* Valley Forge, Penn: Judson Press. Mitchell has compiled twenty-one sermons by African-American preachers seeking to advance female leadership and ministry.

MORGAN, TIMOTHY C.

1981 "The Stained Glass Ceiling: Women Clergy Struggle for Legitimacy as They Celebrate Their Call to Pastoral Ministry." *Christianity Today.* May 16, 1994, Volume 38. This brief article explores the acceptance of women pastors in the church and documents the first conference sponsored by Wesleyan/Holiness Women Clergy, International.

NAYLOR, C. W.

1918   *The Gospel Trumpet.* April 25, 1918. Anderson, Ind: The Gospel Trumpet Company. Naylor briefly addresses women in ministry.

NEWELL, ARLO F.

1989   "For Men Only? Breaking a Two-thousand-year-old Tradition." *Vital Christianity.* May 1989, Anderson, Ind: Warner Press. Newell briefly addresses women in ministry in the Church of God.

NUECHTERLEIN, ANNE MARIE and HAHN, CELIA ALLISON

1990   *The Male-Female Church Staff.* New York: The Alban Institute. This book helpfully explores the issue of gender in church staffs. The authors utilize the Myers-Briggs Type Indicator, case studies, and research. Some sample issues include: self-esteem, leadership, roles, communication, and attraction.

PADGETT, ALAN G.

N.D.   "The Scholarship of Patriarchy (On 1 Timothy 2:8–15): A Response to *Women in the Church,* eds. Kostenberger, Schreiner & Baldwin." This article is found on the Christians for Biblical Equality web page www.cbeinternational.org. In this academic article, Padgett puts forth a cogent response to Kostenberger, Schreiner & Baldwin, and defends women in ministry.

PEARSON, SHARON CLARK

1996   "Women in Ministry: A Biblical Vision." *Wesleyan Theological Journal.* Volume 31, Number 1, Spring. (141–170). Pearson writes an outstanding and scholarly summary New Testament based defense of women in ministry.

PHILLIPS, HAROLD L.

1980   "Wives Submit? Three Interpretations …" *Centering on Ministry.* Winter 1980 Volume 5, Number 2, Anderson, IN: The Center For Pastoral Studies Anderson College School of Theology. This brief article explores the role of female submission.

Selected Bibliography

PISTOLE, ELIZABETH

1978   "Changing Times for Women and the Implications for Church and Family." *The Role of Women in Today's World.* Anderson, Ind: Commission on Social Concerns, Church of God. Pistole briefly considers societal trends and their impact upon women and their families.

RICHARDSON, P.

1979   *Paul's Ethic of Freedom.* Philadelphia: Westminster

ROBERTS, BENJAMIN TITUS

1891   *Ordaining Women: Biblical and Historical Insights.* Rochester, NY: Earnest Christian Publishing House. Reproduced 1992. Indianapolis: Light and Life Press. Roberts, founder and bishop of the Free Methodist Church, puts forth an argument for women in ministry.

RUSSELL, LETTY M.

1986   *Feminist Interpretation of the Bible.* Philadelphia: The Westminster Press. Russell compiles thirteen articles written by female scholars exploring feminist perspectives on scripture.

SCANZONI, LETHA DAWSON and HARDESTY, NANCY A.

1986   *All We're Meant to Be: Biblical Feminism For Today.* Nashville: Abingdon Press. The authors explore contemporary women's issues from a biblical perspective. They advocate for equality in the workplace, home, church, and society.

SCHAPER, DONNA

1990   *Common Sense About Men and Women in Ministry.* New York: The Albans Institute. Writing from a pastoral perspective, Schaper explores gender roles and attitudes in ministry.

SCHOLER, DAVID M.

1998 "Galatians 3:28 and the Ministry of Women in the Church." *Theology, News and Notes.* June Issue, pages 19–22. This copy of Scholer's installation address is a reasoned response to traditionalists who limit the scope of Galatians 3:28 to salvation.

SIDDONS, PHILIP

1980 *Speaking Out For Women: A Biblical View.* Valley Forge, Penn: Judson Press. Exploring Greek, Roman and Jewish cultures, Siddons examines biblical texts seeking to advance the status and responsibility of women in church and society.

SMITH, F. G.

1920 "Editorial," *Gospel Trumpet 40* (June 17, 1920):9. Anderson, Ind: Gospel Trumpet Company. This brief editorial illustrates the pro-woman in ministry view of an early Church of God leader.

SMITH, MONT W.

1996 "Keep On Target: A Preaching Lectureship from the First Epistle to Timothy, Instructions on Order and Structure in the Church and Practical Advice for a Young Pastor." Presented March 1996 at First Church of God, Vancouver, Washington. Notes transcribed and edited by Wayne Amondson. (Second Edition). This lecture contains competent biblical scholarship. Some sections concern the issue of women in ministry.

SPENCER, AIDA BESANCON

1979 *Beyond the Curse: Women Called to Ministry.* New York: Thomas Nelson. Spencer puts forth a well-reasoned, biblical argument for women in ministry.

STANLEY, JOHN

2002 "A Theology of Urban Ministry Based on the Wesleyan Quadrilateral." *Wesleyan Theological Journal.* Volume 38. Number 1, Spring. A portion of this essay contains a defense of women in ministry.

STANLEY, SUSIE CUNNINGHAM

1996 *Honoring God's Call: A Celebration of Holiness Women Preachers.* Kansas City: Beacon Hill Press. This book contains five sermons celebrating God's call upon Holiness women preachers. It explores various elements of the call. It is a good resource for women reflecting upon their calling.

1996 "The Promise Fulfilled: Women's Ministries in the Wesleyan/Holiness Movement," in *Religious Institutions and Women's Leadership: New Roles Inside the Mainstream.* Columbia, SC: University of South Carolina Press. This chapter explores the lives and teachings of selected Wesleyan/Holiness ministers. The article includes a biblical defense for women in ministry.

2002 *Holy Boldness: Women Preachers' Autobiographies and the Sanctified Self.* Knoxville: The University of Tennessee Press. Utilizing biographies, this scholarly work explores the role of sanctification in shaping the lives and ministries of early holiness women preachers. The autobiographies are informative and the section on sanctification is theologically stimulating.

2003 *Wesleyan/Holiness Women Clergy.* www.messiah.edu/whwc. This outstanding Web site is loaded with useful resources.

STERNER, R. EUGENE

1978 "Women in the Church of God" in *The Role of Women in Today's World.* Anderson, Ind: Commission on Social Concerns, Church of God. Sterner suggests that women are not properly represented as decision makers in the Church of God.

STRAUCH, ALEXANDER

1981 *Men and Women Equal Yet Different: A Brief Study of the Biblical Passages on Gender.* Littleton, Colo: Lewis and Roth Publishers. This book puts forth the complementarian argument against women in pastoral ministry. The argument appears reasonable but fails because it does not recognize the firmly imbedded patriarchal bias in its hermeneutics and one could scarcely call a person equal who is permanently barred from leadership.

STREGE, MERLE D.

1989   "Go Ahead, Sister Cole: Where Only Men Had Gone Before" in *Vital Christianity*. May 1989. Anderson, Ind: Warner Press. Strege briefly remembers Sister Mary Cole's ministry in the Church of God.

SWIDLER, LEONARD

1979   *Biblical Affirmations of Woman.* Philadelphia: The Westminster Press.

THURSTON, BONNIE

1998   *Women in the New Testament.* New York: Crossroad.

TRUEBLOOD, D. ELTON

1980   "The Place of Women in the Christian Cause." *Centering on Ministry.* Winter 1980 Volume 5, Number 2, Anderson, Ind: The Center For Pastoral Studies, Anderson College School of Theology. Trueblood makes a brief but impassioned appeal for the church to accept women in ministry.

TUCKER, RUTH A., and LIEFIELD, WALTER

1987   *Daughters of the Church: Women and Ministry from New Testament Times to the Present.* Grand Rapids: Academic Books, Zondervan. The title is self-explanatory.

WARNER, D. S.

1987   "Woman's Freedom in Christ, to Pray and Prophesy in Public Worship." *The Gospel Trumpet* (1 October). This article expresses Warner's acceptance of women in ministry.

WILLIAMS, LIMA LEHMER

1986   *Walking in Missionary Shoes: (1905–1970) A History of the Church of God in East Africa.* Anderson, Ind: Warner Press. Based upon missionary service in Kenya from 1936–1970, Williams pens an informative and inspirational account.

Selected Bibliography

WINNER, LAUREN F.

1997 "The Man Behind the Megachurch." *Christianity Today* (November 13). This article explores the contribution of Gilbert Bilezikian to the Willow Creek Church in Barrington, Illinois. Of particular note is Bilezikian's influence on the emphatic stand in favor of women in ministry at Willow Creek.

ZIKMUND, BARBARA BROWN, LUMMIS, ADAIR T,. and CHANG, PATRICIA M.Y.

1998 *Clergy Women: An Uphill Calling.* Louisville, Ky: Westminster John Knox Press. This comprehensive study explores the issues that women pastors face in today's world. The statistics from fifteen protestant denominations shed significant light upon a broad spectrum of issues and challenges faced by women clergy.

APPENDIX A

Questionnaire for Female Church of God Ministers

My name is Randal Huber. I serve on the Women In Ministry Task Force of the Church of God. This confidential questionnaire is a data-gathering tool studying the placement of licensed and ordained women in the Church of God. The data will be utilized in a Doctor of Ministry project for Anderson University School of Theology. Data summary will be included in a book that will have wide distribution in the Church of God. I would really appreciate a few minutes of your time. You may complete this survey by typing in your response on the underscore next to each question/response. (Note: 'X' or 1–5 as indicated). You can email me with questions at Chapelhill@pa.net. The results of this survey are being gathered to one email account for data entry. Please reply to or email all completed surveys to phobbs@blazenet.net. Thank you for your prompt assistance.

1. Current Ministry Classification: (Check only one.)

_____ Solo/Senior pastor of a Church of God congregation with average Sunday

Morning attendance ____ 2–50 ____ 51–100 ____ 101–200 ____ 201+

_____ Solo/senior pastor of a non-Church of God congregation
_____ Associate pastor of a Church of God congregation
_____ Associate pastor of a non-Church of God congregation
_____ Co-pastor with my husband
_____ Educator, missionary, chaplain, counselor, or para church minister
_____ Church of God district, state, or national leader
_____ Retired/disabled

APPENDIX A

_____ Seeking placement
_____ On temporary professional leave
_____ Ministry Volunteer

2. Employment status: (Check only one.)

   More than 40 hours per week in professional ministry ___
   20–39 hours per week in professional ministry ___
   Less than 20 hours per week in professional ministry ___
   Non-paid volunteer ministry ___

3. Race: (Check only one.)

   African-American ___ Asian/Pacific Islander ___
   Caucasian ___ Hispanic ___ Native American ___
   Other_____

4. Age: 20–30 ___ 31–40 ___ 41–50 ___ 51–60 ___ 61+ ___

5. Highest Educational Attainment (Check only one.)

   High School ___ Bachelors ___ Masters ___ Doctorate ___

6. The last time you sought ministerial placement in the Church of God

   0–5 years ago ___ 6–10 years ago ___ Over 10 years ago ___

PLEASE USE THE FOLLOWING SCALE FOR THE REMAINING QUESTIONS:

1—Strongly Agree   2—Agree   3—Undecided
4—Disagree   5—Strongly Disagree

7. ____ My attempts at ministerial placement in the Church of God have been highly positive.

8. ____ My female gender has had no significant impact upon my ministerial placement in the Church of God.

9. _____ I am called to professional ministry, but I have been unable to find a position in the Church of God commensurate with my education and gifts.

10. _____ My Area Administrator or Ministerial Credentials Committee was highly involved in finding placement for me.

11. _____ My Church of God educational institution took every reasonable step in helping me find ministerial placement (Leave this question blank if you did not attend a Church of God college or seminary).

12. _____ I am highly satisfied with the assistance of the Congregational Ministries Team of Church of God Ministries in seeking placement for me (Leave this question blank if you did not submit a brief to Congregational Ministries).

13. _____ A mentor or church leader has advocated for me to assist me in finding placement.

COMMENTS: I am writing a book that will utilize this data. If you have anecdotal incidents, comments or observations that you would like for me to consider for inclusion, I would appreciate what you have to say. As this survey is confidential, I will not disclose identifying information. Thank you.

APPENDIX B

Overall Survey Response

AVERAGE ANSWER:

Q#7	Q#8	Q#9	Q#10	Q#11	Q#12	Q#13
2.52	3.04	3.67	3.53	3.53	3.38	2.74

Total Records 241

Education

High School:	67	28%
Bachelors:	86	36%
Masters:	70	29%
Doctorate:	14	06%
Answered:	237	98%

Employment Status

Non-Paid Volunteer	80	33%
Less than 20 Hours:	34	14%
20–39 Hours:	35	15%
40+ Hours:	70	29%
Answered:	219	91%

Age

20-30:	7	03%
31-40:	34	14%
41–50:	72	30%
51–60:	55	23%
61+:	69	29%
Answered:	237	98%

Sought Placement

0–5 years ago:	111	46%
6–10 years ago:	30	12%
10+ years ago:	50	21%
Answered:	191	79%

Developer: Peter B. Hobbs
Date: 02/05/2003

INDEX

General Index

A

adultery 29, 46, 49, 72, 75
Africa 11, 33, 93, 114, 130, 136
ambassadors 19-20, 22
Anderson 10, 13, 84, 87, 99-100, 114-117, 119-121, 123-130
Anderson University 3, 11, 13, 82, 87, 115, 121, 132
Apostle 10, 18, 20, 27, 50-51, 54, 64, 74
apostles 10, 41, 47, 49, 54-55
area administrator 134
authority authority 8, 10, 16-17, 19, 22, 35, 39, 50, 58-63, 65, 68, 72-74, 77, 96, 99, 106, 116, 125

B

Bible 2, 7-17, 29, 34, 50-51, 54, 64-65, 71-72, 74, 83, 85, 87, 93, 96-98, 102, 104, 117-120, 122, 124-125, 127
biblical 3, 7-14, 16-17, 21, 23, 51-52, 55, 59-60, 65-66, 70-72, 77, 89-90, 97-102, 104, 107, 110-112, 115-120, 122-130
biblical equality 51-52, 55, 59, 98, 102, 104, 122, 126
bishop 127
bylaws 11-12, 107

C

call 7-8, 10-11, 16, 34-35, 41, 48, 68, 76, 79, 82, 84, 86-89, 93, 97, 99-100, 104, 107-109, 111, 119, 125, 129
called 1, 4, 7-8, 10-12, 16, 18, 20-22, 24, 26, 28, 30, 34-38, 40, 42, 44, 46, 48, 52, 54, 56, 58, 60-62, 64, 68-70, 72, 74, 76, 80, 82-84, 86-88, 90, 92-93, 103-105, 109, 112, 115, 123, 128, 134
Chapel Hill Church of God 3-4, 11, 69, 85, 107
Christian Holiness Partnership 13
Church 1-2, 4, 7-24, 26, 28-30, 34, 36, 38, 40-42, 44, 46-48, 50-58, 60-65, 67-70, 72, 74-78, 80-90, 92-94, 96, 98-106, 108-111, 114-121, 123, 125-128, 130-132, 134
Church of God 5, 10-11, 13, 17, 70, 80-90, 93-94, 98-100, 105-110, 113-117, 120-121, 123-130, 132-134
Church of the Nazarene 99-100, 116, 123
context 8-9, 20, 34, 56-59, 62-63, 75, 106, 122

General Index

created 3, 23-27, 30-31, 33-34, 41, 62-63, 71-72, 74, 98, 100, 104
creation 12, 19, 24-26, 28-30, 34, 41, 45, 71, 98
crucifixion 47
curse 24, 28, 30, 34, 38-39, 41, 45-46, 48, 71-72, 128

D

deacon 8, 15-16, 21, 52-53
deceived 15, 24, 27, 31, 63
deception 27
descriptive 9, 29, 31
diakonos 8, 53
disciple 15
disciples 17, 40, 42-44, 47, 49, 105
district 13, 132
divine image 25, 27, 31, 34, 41, 98, 104
dominance 29-30, 33-34
dominion 24-25, 27, 30-31, 34, 41, 71, 98

E

elders 11-12
Ephesus 9, 53, 60-63
Episcopal 10, 108, 114, 118
equal 25-26, 30, 34, 41, 52, 54, 68, 71, 80, 98, 118, 122, 124, 129
equality 9, 25, 51-52, 55, 59, 97-98, 100-102, 104, 111-112, 120, 122, 126-127
equipped 1, 4, 7-8, 10, 12, 16, 18, 20-21, 24, 26, 28, 30, 34, 36-38, 42, 44, 46, 48, 52, 54, 56, 58, 60, 62, 64, 68, 70, 72, 74, 76, 80, 82, 84, 86-88, 90, 92, 103, 112
evangelical 11
experience 10-11, 14, 17, 27, 64, 82-83, 86, 88-89, 92, 105
ezer kenegdo 25-26

F

fall 12, 23-24, 27-30, 33-34, 41, 45, 70-72, 74, 77, 101
female 5, 8, 10, 12, 16, 20-21, 24-26, 34, 38-39, 42, 47, 50-52, 54-55, 59, 62-64, 69-70, 75-77, 79-80, 84-85, 89, 93-96, 99-101, 103, 105, 107-110, 112, 117-118, 125-127, 132-133
feminism 96-102, 117, 127
feminist 5, 96-98, 101, 127
Free Methodist 37, 127
foreign languages 18-19
fundamentalist 11, 106, 116

G

gender 5, 15-17, 19, 21-22, 34-35, 53, 60, 79, 83-84, 86, 95-96, 98, 100-101, 107-109, 119-120, 122, 126-127, 129, 133
Gentiles 52
gender-based leadership 16, 22, 34
gifts 5, 7, 11, 15-22, 29, 36, 40-41, 48, 55, 57-58, 64, 67-69, 72, 75, 88, 90, 93, 98-100, 104, 107-109, 111, 134
Gnostic 62-63
Gnosticism 9, 62
Gospel Trumpet 17, 80, 94, 100, 126, 128, 130

H

head 36, 56, 73-75, 77
headship 8, 66, 73-74, 77, 123
helper 23, 25-27, 31, 118
heritage 12, 14, 16, 82, 105, 112, 121
hierarchical 73
hierarchy 10, 24-28, 34, 41, 71-72, 98
history 8, 11, 27, 29, 33-34, 47-48, 51, 80-81, 97, 105, 107, 111, 114, 117, 121, 124-125, 130
Holy Spirit 14, 17-19, 21-22, 37, 44, 79-80, 83, 88-89, 100, 103-104, 112
husband 24, 28, 33-34, 37, 44, 53-54, 58, 66, 69, 71-73, 81, 84-85, 88, 90, 114, 132

I

image 24-26, 74
interpretation 8, 14, 52, 106, 125, 127

K

Kephale 73-74, 77

L

leader 8-9, 17, 32, 35-36, 39, 41, 53-55, 73-74, 79, 81-83, 87-88, 90, 100, 110, 128, 132, 134
leaders 7, 10-14, 32, 34-39, 42, 47-48, 51-55, 59, 62-65, 69, 76, 79-80, 82, 85, 87, 94-95, 100-101, 104-105, 107-108, 110, 113, 115, 117, 121, 123
leadership 7-8, 11-12, 16-17, 21-22, 28, 32-36, 38, 47, 49, 52-53, 55, 57, 59-60, 63, 69, 82, 84-85, 93-94, 96, 99, 104, 106-108, 110-111, 113, 117-118, 121, 124-126, 129
Louisville Institute 13

M

male 8, 10, 12-14, 20-21, 24-27, 29-30, 33-34, 36, 40, 42-43, 45-47, 49, 51-54, 59, 63-64, 66, 70, 72-77, 79-80, 85, 96, 99-101, 103, 110, 112, 123, 126
male covering 66, 72, 74
male headship 8, 73-74, 77, 123
men 5, 7-10, 13-42, 45, 47-48, 50-51, 53, 56-60, 62-63, 66-68, 71-72, 74-75, 77-80, 87, 90, 93-100, 104, 108, 110-111, 122, 126-127, 129-130
Mid-America Bible College 13
minister 8, 21, 42, 46, 53, 86, 89, 103, 105, 108-110, 115, 123-124, 132
ministers 5, 13, 51, 85-86, 88, 105-110, 116, 123, 129, 132
ministry 9-12, 19-21, 23, 42, 45, 48, 51-52, 55, 58-60, 64, 66-70, 72, 75, 78, 80, 90, 93-95, 97-99, 101, 104, 106-112, 115-121, 123-134
monogamous 9

N

National Organization for Women 100

O

Obedience 21, 112
Oberlin College 99

P

particular 9, 17, 57, 60, 63, 65, 75, 77, 100, 108, 117, 131
pastor 3, 7-8, 11-12, 15-16, 23-24, 32, 38, 40-41, 48, 50, 61, 64, 66, 69-70, 72, 74, 76-78, 80-89, 93-94, 100, 104-106, 109-110, 112-115, 119, 128, 132
pastors 1, 3-4, 7-8, 10-16, 18, 20, 22, 24, 26, 28, 30-31, 34, 36, 38, 42, 44, 46, 48, 52, 54, 56, 58-62, 64-66, 68-70, 72, 74-78, 80-82, 84, 86, 88, 90, 92-96, 102-107, 109-110, 112-113, 115-116, 119-121, 124-125, 131
patriarchal 34, 48, 53-54, 85, 111, 129
patriarchy 29, 31, 33-34, 36, 38-41, 43, 45, 47, 60, 71-72, 106, 110, 126
Point Loma Nazarene University 13
preach 9, 11, 16, 19, 21, 24, 29, 38, 44, 47, 56, 74, 88, 90, 104-105, 109-110, 117, 123, 125
preacher 15, 79, 85, 88, 99
preachers 16, 18, 22, 38, 47, 49, 51, 68, 99-100, 105, 109, 125, 129
preaching 16, 18, 35, 47, 55-56, 58, 63, 68, 70, 80-81, 85, 88, 93, 105, 117, 128
prescriptive 9, 29, 31
priest 10, 36, 87, 108
prophecy 16, 18, 35, 55-56, 59, 88
prophesy 17-19, 22, 36, 39, 56-57, 65, 130
prophesy, 61
prophet 18-19, 27, 35-37, 39
prophets 19, 36, 38, 55

Q

quadrilateral 14, 128
questionnaire 5, 132

R

racism 28, 111, 113
racist 43-44, 111
radical feminism 98
reason 10, 12, 14, 27, 61
reconciliation 19, 45, 111
resurrected 47
Roman Catholic 8
rule 5, 9, 23-25, 27-30, 34, 53, 71, 98

S

Salvation Army 35, 99, 117
Samaritan 43-44
servant 8, 48, 53, 71
sex 12, 16-18, 20-21, 40, 71, 90, 99, 117
sexism 68, 111, 113
sexist 5, 40-41, 43-48, 108, 111
silence 50, 57-58, 61, 63, 106
silent 39, 50, 57-58, 63, 65
sin 5, 9, 27-30, 33-34, 36, 38-39, 41, 45-46, 71-72, 103-105, 107, 109, 111, 113
Southern Baptist 8
Spirit 16, 18, 20-21, 40, 48, 51-52, 80
spiritual gifts 15-16, 18, 20-22, 29, 40, 48, 55, 57-58, 67-69, 72, 75, 88, 90, 98, 107-108, 111

subjugation 28-29, 31, 34, 41

―――― T ――――

teach 7, 16, 21-22, 24, 39, 41-45, 50, 58, 60-61, 63, 87, 104, 110
tradition 10, 14, 43, 99, 126
tradition, 14

―――― U ――――

unclean 45-46, 49
universal 9, 57, 59-60, 62-63
upper room 17
usurp 60-61, 63, 90

―――― V ――――

veil 9, 74
Vital Christianity 80, 108, 115, 120, 124, 126, 130

―――― W ――――

Warner Pacific College 13
Wesleyan/Holiness 12, 14, 68, 99, 106, 110, 118, 121, 125, 129
wife 3, 15, 28, 35-36, 42, 53, 67, 69-73, 80, 84
woman 5, 7-8, 11-12, 16-17, 19, 21, 23-29, 31-34, 36-38, 40, 42-46, 48-51, 53-59, 61-64, 66-68, 71-72, 74, 78-91, 93-94, 97, 100, 104, 106, 108-109, 112-113, 117-119, 122, 124, 128, 130
women 1, 3-4, 7-52, 54-72, 74-82, 84-90, 92-132

Biographical Index

A

Aaron 35, 39, 69
Abraham 32, 71
Adam 23, 25-28, 38, 63, 73, 118, 125
Allison, Joseph 17, 81
Anna 12, 34, 37-39, 59, 80-81, 104
Apollos 53-54
Aquila 53-54
Armstrong, Don 85

B

Barwick, Burd 81
Bathsheba 72
Baumgardner, Jennifer 97
Berry, Barbara 87-88
Booth, Catherine 35, 37, 99, 118
Bilezikian, Gilbert 20, 25, 72-73, 131
Bosconer, Mamie 81
Boyer, Esther 81
Brooks, Wilma 88
Brown, Amanda 81
Brown, C. E. 93
Brown, Dana B. 82, 114
Brown, Viola 81
Burcher, William 4
Burgess, Emma 81

C

Callen, Barry 70, 81
Carter, Gertrude 81
Charles, Lottie 81
Chloe 55, 59
Chuza 42
Clark, Adam 38
Cobb, Judy 4
Cottrell, Esther 80
Coulbourne, Emma 81
Cowles, C. S. 8, 14, 33, 98
Craft, Tillie 81
Crew, Louie 114

D

David 9, 32, 72, 128
Deborah 12, 34-39, 59, 104
Decker, Ted 4
Diana 61, 63
Duncan, Mrs. T. A. 81

E

Eldred, John 119
Euodia 54-55, 59
Evans, Mary 42
Eve 23, 26-28, 48, 63, 73

F

Farmer, Lura 81
Flynn, Jeannette 80, 82
Frazee, May 81

G

Gaulke, Bertha 81
Goode, Richard 21, 92, 110
Guilford, L. W. and Claudine 81

H

Hardesty, Nancy A. 127
Harding, Leslie 108
Harkness, Georgia 67

Hawkins, Mary Ann 84-85, 105, 114
Helpingstone 11
Henry, Marilyn 105
Hinzman, Flora 11
Hobbs, Peter 3, 106
Huber, Janice Elaine 3
Huldah 34, 36-39, 59, 104
Hull, Gretchen Gaebelin 20
Hunter, Nora S. 81

I

Ingersol, Stan 99
Isaac, Kim 4
Isaac 32, 71

J

Jacob 9, 26, 32, 44, 72
James, Cynthia 88
Joanna 42
Joe, Hyunhye Pkrifka 20, 22
Johnson, Rita J. 91
Josiah 36
Judas 17
Julia 52, 59
Junia 52, 54, 59, 104

K

Keener, Craig 74
Kemp, Pearl 81
Kilpatrick, Rose 81
Koglin, Anna E. 80
Kroeger, Catherine 63
Kroeger, Richard 60, 62

L

Lamech 28
Lavell, Effie 81
Leah 72

Lehman, Edward C. 68, 111
Lehmer, Lima 11, 114, 130
LeMay, Mike 4, 69
Leonard, Juanita 3, 33, 105, 115, 123, 130
Liefield, Walter L. 56
Longenecker, Richard 56
Lydia 55, 59, 104

M

Mallett, Sarah 99
Mary, the mother of Jesus 17
Martha 43
Mary 17, 42-43, 47-49, 52, 55, 84-85, 104-105, 114, 119-120, 130
Massey, James Earl 82
Matthesen, Leno Shoffner 81
Matthias 17
Maxwell, Pauline 81
May, Grace Ying 20, 22
McAlpine, Mae 81
McCain, Sarah Massey 81
McCracken, Beth Harness 3
McCutcheon, Lillie 70, 81-82, 84
Mickelsen, Alvera 73
Miles, Rosalind 33, 55
Miller, Barbara Deale 89-90, 114
Miriam 12, 34-35, 37-39, 59, 104
Moses 32, 35, 39
Myers, Emma and Willa 81

N

Naylor, C. W. 80
Neal, Hazel G. 81
Newell, Arlo 108
Nympha 55

Biographical Index

O

Onesimus 52

P

Padgett, Alan G. 62
Parkins, Ada B. 81
Paul 5, 8-10, 12, 18, 20, 27, 50-65, 74, 83, 101, 106, 116, 122-123, 125, 127
Pauley, Sydney and Delcie 81
Payne, Philip Barton 73
Pearson, Sharon Clark 3, 46, 61
Persis 52, 59
Philemon 52
Philip 55, 73, 128
Phoebe 8, 12, 52-53, 59, 104
Poiner, Sarah 88
Prisca 55
Priscilla 32, 52-54, 59, 104, 124
Pye, Dassie M. 81
Pythagoras 33

R

Rabbi Eliezer 41, 43
Rachel 72, 81
Rawlinson, Rachel Bailey 81
Reed, L. 81
Reid, Carolyn Waddy 84, 114
Rennick, Steve 85
Richards, Amy 97
Roberts, Benjamin Titus 37, 46, 52, 61
Rothman, Zuda Chambers 81
Rowe, Bertha 81

S

Sanders, Cheryl 90-93, 114
Sarah 71, 81, 88, 98
Scanzoni, Letha Dawson 127
Schaffer, Marie 81
Shelton, Naomi 81
Simeon 37
Slaybaugh, Jeannine 4
Smith, F. G. 17, 100
Solomon 72
Sprague, Alice 81
Stanley, John 3-4, 12-14, 99-100
Stanley, Mandy 85, 87, 114
Stanley, Susie 3, 10, 52, 68, 85, 99, 106
Stanton, Elizabeth Cady 99
Strauch, Alexander 52
Susanna 42
Swidler, Leonard 33
Syntyche 54-55, 59

T

Taft, Rev. Dr. 61
Tires, Willa Mae 88
Thompson, Marianne Meye 19
Tosh, S. J. 81
Trask, Edith A. 81
Trueblood, D. Elton 105
Tryphena 52, 59
Tryphosa 52, 59

U

Uriah the Hittite 72

W

Wallace 11
Wantz, Harold 4
Warner, D. S. 80
Weber, Timothy P. 7
Wesley, John 98
Williams, Jane 81
Winner, Lauren 20
Woodhull, Victoria 100

Scripture Index

Genesis 1:26–28	24
Genesis 2:16–17	27
Genesis 2:18	23, 25
Genesis 2:21–22	23
Genesis 3:16–19	28
Genesis 3:16	24, 28, 71
Genesis 5:1–2	25
Genesis 16	71
Genesis 24	71
Genesis 29:20	72
Genesis 29	72
Exodus 15:20–21	35
Leviticus 15:19	45
Leviticus 20:10	46
Deuteronomy 21:10–14	72
Deuteronomy 24:1–4	72
Deuteronomy 25:5–10	29
Deuteronomy 25:5–6	72
Judges 4:1–5	35
Ruth 4:10	72
2 Samuel 11	72
1 Kings 11:11	72
1 Kings 19:1–2	27
2 Kings 22:14–16	36
Psalm 146:5	26
Psalm 68:11	37
Hosea 3:2	72
Micah 6:4	35
Matthew 5:27–28	46
Matthew 5:31–32	72
Matthew 7:13–14	105
Matthew 9:20–22	45
Matthew 19:3–9	46
Matthew 27:55–56	47
Matthew 27:59–61	47
Matthew 28:1–10	47
Mark 15:47	47
Mark 16:1–9	47
Luke 1:46–48	48
Luke 2:36–38	37
Luke 8:1–3	42
Luke 10:38–42	43
Luke 16:18	72
Luke 23:49	47
Luke 23:55–56	47
Luke 24:1–10	47
John 4:25–42	44
John 8:1–11	46
John 19:25–27	47
John 20:1–18	47
Acts 1:4–5	17
Acts 1:14	17-18
Acts 1:15	17
Acts 2:1–2	17
Acts 2:4	18
Acts 2:5–11	19
Acts 2:16–18	18
Acts 18:18	54
Acts 18:26	54
Acts 18:24–26	53
Acts 21:8–9	55
Romans 7:11	27
Romans 12:4–8	20
Romans 16:1–2	52
Romans 16:21	54
Romans 16:3	54
Romans 16:7	54
1 Corinthians 1:11	55
1 Corinthians 3:9	54
1 Corinthians 11:1–16	73

Scripture Index

1 Corinthians 11:3–16	56
1 Corinthians 12:4–26	20
1 Corinthians 14:1–5	18
1 Corinthians 14:33–36	9, 50, 57
2 Corinthians 5:16–20	19
2 Corinthians 5:17–19	45
2 Corinthians 8:23	54
Galatians 3:28	112, 128
Galatians 5:22–23	79
Ephesians 2:8–9	60
Ephesians 4:11–12	20
Ephesians 5:21–33	73
Philippians 4:2–3	54
Colossians 3:18–19	73
1 Timothy 1:3–7	62
1 Timothy 1:7	62
1 Timothy 2:1–3	62
1 Timothy 2:8–9	63
1 Timothy 2:8–10	59
1 Timothy 2:11–12	63
1 Timothy 2:13–15	63
1 Timothy 2:15	60
1 Timothy 3:8–12	53
2 Timothy 3:16	8
2 Timothy 4:19	54
2 Peter 1:20–21	8
2 Peter 3:9	104